CW01501125

About the Author

David Boswell was born in 1927 in Bickley, Kent (now part of the London conurbation), the son of a doctor, and educated at Epsom College. Following this he studied dentistry at Guys Hospital, qualifying in 1949. He then served his "two year sentence" of National Service as a Dental Officer at R.A.F. Pembroke Dock, among the Sunderland flying boats. After a move to North Somerset he spent almost forty five years in general dental practice, retiring in 1997. He is married to Joan, and they have two sons and two daughters, and four grandchildren. During the 90's he studied for an Open University degree, following the geological subjects, and he is also interested in archaeology. So having all his life been interested in scientific matters, he has considerably surprised himself by writing this book with a more literary theme. As Rossini put it so well, " a sin of old age," perhaps.

He has been the genealogical "Boswell of Auchinleck" since 1969.

My Very Dearest
Sweet Heart

or

Boswell

Before

Boswell

Letters of the Lady Elizabeth Boswell
(1704 to 1711, and 1733)

Life before the Biographer

by

David R. Boswell

OXMUIR SCRIPT
BATH

[Oxmuir .. Ye Place (in Berwickshire) where ye Bosvilles first settled in Scotland]

Published in 2003 by

Oxmuir Script
Balmuto
Bath BA2 0HD

All rights reserved. No part of this publication may be reproduced,
stored in a retrieval system, or transmitted in any form, or by any means,
electronic, mechanical, photocopying, recording or otherwise, without
the prior permission of the publisher.

A CIP catalogue record for this book
is available from the British Library.

ISBN 0-9545347-0-0

Copyright © David Boswell 2003

Printed by
Antony Rowe
Chippenham
SN14 6LH

First Edition, 2003, 500 copies

PLATE 1 : JAMES BOSWELL 7TH OF AUCHINLECK
(1672-1749)

PLATE 2 : LADY ELIZABETH BOSWELL
(née BRUCE) (1671-1739)

Foreword

It has been a privilege to read the letters of my forebear Lady Elizabeth Boswell. The reason for her diligence over so many years was the Lang Whang[1], the lonely, dreich[2] and, at times, windswept road which runs from her Ayrshire home to Edinburgh. She preferred not to make this journey too often but have recourse to her pen. On almost every occasion she writes, she made the point of choosing and naming the courier of the letter.

Like so many wives of Lairds she mistressed the art of good motherhood, housekeeping, farming, the creation of woodlands and the handling of a vegetable garden. She obviously enjoyed the gossip of neighbours and was very diligent in her promotion, through several churches, of a very refreshing attitude to the discipline of her own Christian Faith.

---

(1) Whang = 1) Thong 2) Slice 3) A blow or rather a lash with a whip (perhaps this applies to effect of the weather on one)
(2) Dreich = 1) slow 2) tedious or wearisome

David Boswell has also created a most valuable historical skeleton to the letters. This will help those not so deeply imbued in the Bruce, Boswell and Cochrane families to understand how important these family ties could be in the late 17th and early 18th centuries.

The Earl of Elgin and Kincardine K.T.

ACKNOWLEDGEMENTS

I owe grateful thanks to many people who have researched into, or put me on the right track for various pieces of necessary information or illustration. They include:-

- Rosemary Harden, Naomi Tarrant, and Rhian Tritton, The Fashion Research Centre, Bath.
- John Edwards, Trustee, Bath Postal Museum.
- Dr. Stephen Lloyd, Senior Curator, Scottish National Portrait Gallery.
- Ian Nelson, Edinburgh Room, Edinburgh Central Library.
- David Easton, Royal Commission on the Ancient and Historical Monuments of Scotland.
- Marion Lynch, Archives Assistant, and Huw Pritchard Assistant Archivist, Ayrshire Archive Centre, Ayr.
- Jeanette Castle, Carnegie Librarian, Carnegie Library, Ayr.
- Iain Milne and Estela Dukan, Librarians, Royal College of Physicians, Edinburgh.
- Irene Ferguson, Assistant to University Archivist, Edinburgh University Library.
- Moira Rankin, Senior Archivist, University of Glasgow.
- Ruraidh Wishart, Search Room Archivist, National Archives of Scotland.
- Chris Reekie, General Records of Scotland, Edinburgh.

- Anne Geddes, Community Librarian (Heritage Services), East Ayrshire Council, Cumnock.
- Andrea Longson, Senior Librarian, The Faculty of Advocates, Edinburgh.
- Neil Gow, Q.C., Sheriff of Ayr.

Also to the Right Hon. The Earl of Elgin and Kincardine, K.T., for his kind foreword, and together with Margaret Boswell Eliott, and James Irvine Fortescue for family information of great value. And our sons, Robert for his resumé of English and Scottish history around the turn of the seventeenth and eighteenth centuries, and Andrew for his invaluable computer skills. As also our neighbour and friend Douglas Taviner for his assistance in transcribing the illustrations into computer disc format, and our friend Jeanne Warwick, who from her embroidery knowledge and skills suggested a possible explanation for "stamping."

And finally to Joan my wife who has tolerated my near obsession with Lady Elizabeth's letters and the study and research involved over the past year or so, in much of which she herself has given me much valuable help. Indeed I felt that she should be included as an author, but this she declined. I fear our writing styles are so different we should nearly have come to blows had she agreed !

CONTENTS

PLATES

1). JAMES BOSWELL 7TH OF AUCHINLECK (1672-1749)
2). LADY ELIZABETH BOSWELL (née BRUCE) (1671-1739)
3). AUCHINLECK OLD PLACE (PRINT OF 1791)
4). VERONICA COUNTESS OF KINCARDINE (née VAN SOMMELSDYCK) (1633 – 1701)
5). ALEXANDER BRUCE 2ND EARL OF KINCARDINE (1629 – 1680)
6). LUCIA VAN SOMMELSDYCK (née DE WALTA)
7). CORNELIUS VAN AERSSEN VAN SOMMELSDYCK
8). DAVID BOSWELL, 6TH OF AUCHINLECK (1640-1713)
9). ANNA BOSWELL (née HAMILTON) (1640-1711)
10). SOLE LETTER IN JAMES' HANDWRITING
11). VERONICA BOSWELL (1705-?)
12). ALEXANDER BOSWELL 8TH OF AUCHINLECK, LORD AUCHINLECK (1707-1782)
13). JOHN BOSWELL MD (1710-1780) IN PRESIDENTIAL ROBE OF WHAT LATER BECAME THE ROYAL COLLEGE OF PHYSICIANS OF EDINBURGH
14). BAPTISMAL ENTRY OF PREVIOUSLY UNKNOWN SON DAVID
15). LADY ELIZABETH'S PRAYER BOOK TITLE PAGE AND SIGNATURE
16). PSALM 23

Some portraits are unfortunately reproduced from poor quality source images, which was regrettable but unavoidable. However, despite this, it is felt that a poor image is better than no image.

THE BOSWELL FAMILY TREE

FOR THE LATER SEVENTEENTH AND EARLY EIGHTEENTH CENTURIES

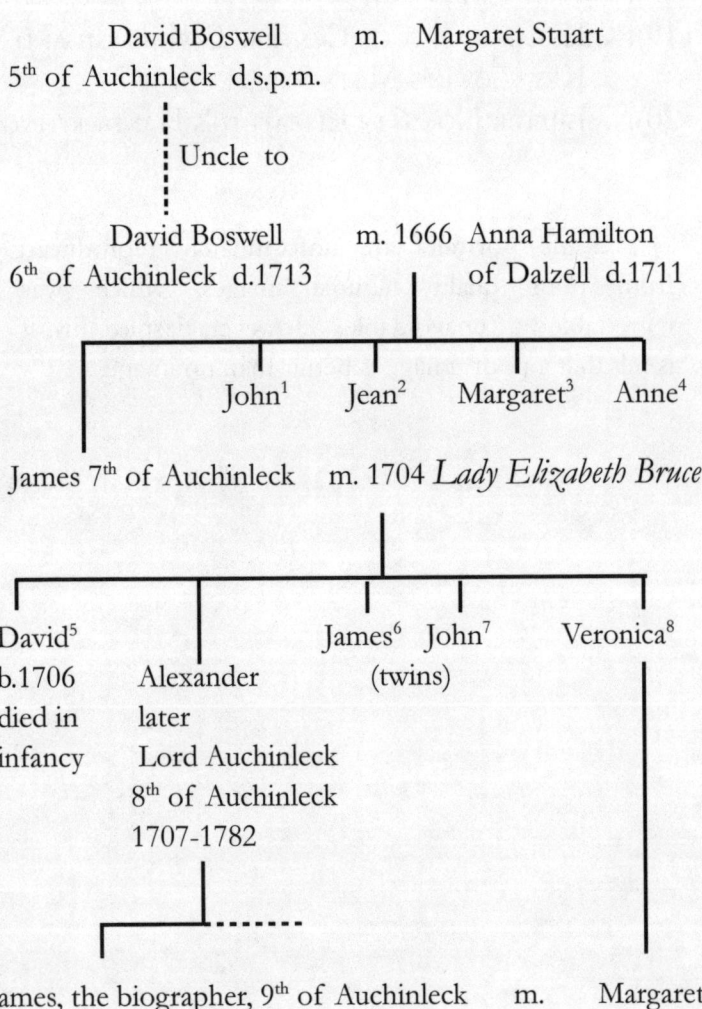

David Boswell   m.   Margaret Stuart
5th of Auchinleck   d.s.p.m.

    Uncle to

David Boswell   m. 1666   Anna Hamilton
6th of Auchinleck   d.1713   of Dalzell   d.1711

John[1]   Jean[2]   Margaret[3]   Anne[4]

James 7th of Auchinleck   m. 1704 *Lady Elizabeth Bruce*

David[5]   James[6] John[7]   Veronica[8]
b.1706   Alexander   (twins)
died in   later
infancy   Lord Auchinleck
          8th of Auchinleck
          1707-1782

James, the biographer, 9th of Auchinleck   m.   Margaret

Lady Elizabeth Bruce's parents and grandparents

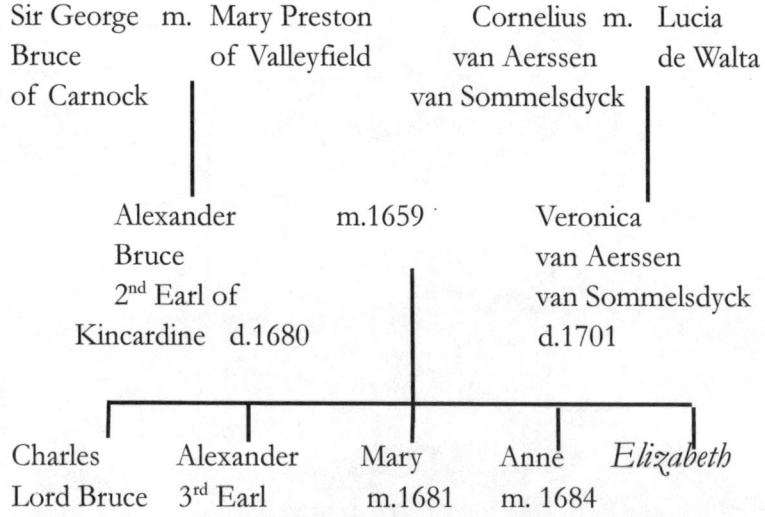

Sir George m. Mary Preston   Cornelius m. Lucia
Bruce   of Valleyfield   van Aerssen   de Walta
of Carnock   van Sommelsdyck

Alexander   m.1659   Veronica
Bruce   van Aerssen
2nd Earl of   van Sommelsdyck
Kincardine   d.1680   d.1701

Charles   Alexander   Mary   Anne   *Elizabeth*
Lord Bruce   3rd Earl   m.1681   m. 1684

Notes:
1. John purchased Balmuto (1726) from his kinsman Andrew Boswell 10th of Balmuto to become 11th of Balmuto
2. Jean (d.s.p 1698) m. 1697 John Campbell 8th of Horsecleugh
3. Margaret m.? Hugh Campbell of Barquharrie
4. Anne m.? George Campbell of Treesbank
5. David discovered in the letters, before Alexander (see Chapter 2).
6. James W.S. d.unm. . 1757
7. John, M.D., President Royal College of Physicians
8. Veronica married David Montgomerie of Lainshaw. Their daughter Margaret would later become, by a first cousin marriage, the wife of James Boswell the biographer.

PROLOGUE

Thirty years or more ago, the late Gordon Hoyle, the founder and leading light at that time of the Auchinleck Boswell Society, had the somewhat macabre habit of taking visitors to the Museum, in the newly restored Old Kirk in Auchinleck village, into the Boswell family vault beneath, where the interments are arranged rather like a rank of filing cabinets. One in particular had two corners fractured off, deliberately or otherwise, and by judicious use of a torch it was possible to gaze in upon the bones within. It gives one a very weird sensation indeed when the bones are those of ones ancestor!

The ancestor concerned was my eight times grandfather James Boswell, 7th of Auchinleck (who was also grandfather to James Boswell the biographer of Samuel Johnson). We have in our family archive, some ancient letters, on yellowish paper, very fragile, and with frayed edges, but still clearly legible. These were from James senior's wife, the Lady Elizabeth Boswell, née Bruce, to her husband, who as a lawyer had to live and work in Edinburgh during the Court sessions. The one exception is one from James himself to Elizabeth, and as he wrote in a form of the mediaeval "Secretary Hand", extremely difficult to interpret. My father had looked at them and came to the conclusion they were love letters, and too personal to read, but closer examination shows this is not so. The couple did indeed address each other as "My Sweet Dearest" or similar endearments (from whence of course the title of this little book is derived), but the letters are in the main very down to earth, discussing matters concerning the Auchinleck estate, the ministerial situation in the Kirk, purchases James is being asked to make in Edinburgh, and of course their transport, and many family matters, either of their children's health, or their need for clothes, but also much concerning Elizabeth's eldest sister Lady Mary who seems to have had marital problems.

In transcribing the letters I have kept very strictly to Lady Elizabeth's spelling, which can best be described as flexible, and where possible have endeavoured to give translations of the various Scotticisms which appear throughout. I was fortunate in obtaining access to two Scottish Dictionaries, one from Bath Public Library, and it turned out that we had one ourselves among various eighteenth and nineteenth century volumes which have come down the family. These have been recorded where appropriate as S.D.(C.) [Craigie], and S.D.(J.) [Jamieson] respectively - details in Bibliography. While on the subject of flexible spelling – this seems to have been the habit of former times up to just later than this period (for example James junior's spelling is much more consistent than his grandmother's). The name Boswell itself illustrates this quite well – Boswel,

Boswell, Boswall, Bosville all are alternative spellings. Its origin is believed to derive from a village in Normandy named Bosville, meaning "the town near the wood", and from whence our very earliest forebears who accompanied Duke William on his cross-Channel adventure in 1066 are said to have come. Interestingly however, there is a Boswell Farm near Sidmouth in East Devon, and we are told of it that the name derives from the Old English word "bosk", meaning wood – so a similar derivation from both sides of the Channel. .

Later there is mention of Lady Elizabeth's frugality, and this seems to have extended to her use of full stops – many of her sentences become somewhat convoluted.

The first two of the letters date from August 1704 in the early days of James and Elizabeth's marriage (on 26th March, 1704) and are written from Culross, Fife, where Elizabeth was possibly staying with her sister. There is then a gap until 1708, by when Elizabeth is living at Auchinleck (at the "Old Place" of course; the present Auchinleck House was not built until the late 1750's) with her parents-in-law, and seemingly with quite a high degree of responsibility for running the estate. This sequence concludes in February 1711, and there are then a separate group of three, written from Edinburgh in 1733, to her youngest son John (from whom I am descended), who was in the later stages of his medical studies, and preparing to sail to Holland to undertake studies for his doctorate under the Dutch professor William Boerhaave in Leyden.

A final note about the subtitle. When the name Boswell comes into discussion, it is James junior, noted for his biography, the Tour to the Hebrides, the Account of Corsica, and in more recent years perhaps notorious more than noted for some of the content of his Journals, who springs immediately to mind. But we feel very strongly that these letters, written thirty to forty years before James' birth, and containing much fascinating social and family history, deserve publication and recognition.

PLATE 3 (OPPOSITE):
AUCHINLECK OLD PLACE
(PRINT OF 1791)

MY VERY DEAREST SWEET HEART

v

LETTERS NO.1 AND 2 (1704)

No.1.

To

Mr. James Boswell of

Auchinleck Advocat

att Edinburgh

My Dearest

Tho I have not much to trouble you with yet I could
not let this occation pass without writting a line for
since I must be deprived of my Dears comfortable
company (which I much regrart but submit to seeing
God in his providence is pleased to order it so) I
desire to make it up the best way I can in conversing
by writ, since I can do it no other way ; No doubt my
Dearest ther is a need for all we meet with, it may be
my heart would be to much sett upon wer I alone with
you, and therefore I desire to be persuaded that it is
always best as it is, that the Lord orders all things well
and wisely, of the laively faith of that blest promice
that all shall work together for good, we would sure
never be anxious nor inordinately concerned, but
would equally bless God in adversity and prosperity.
My Dearest if your affairs cannot permitt you to
come here upon Saturday I beg you may let me know
by a line with the first occation, if you think
Ocheltrie[3] will soon end with us, and if my Sister said
anything to you upon what I wrot to her.

---

(3) William Cochrane of Ochiltree, husband to Elizabeth's eldest
   sister, Lady Mary.

I hope you made a safe journey to Ed'r, which I shall be glad to hear. Now My Dearest I will give you no further trouble at this time, I pray the peace of God with you, I am

  My Dearest Heart

  Culross August 9   Yours most affectionately

       1704   Eli. Boswell

No.2.

To
Mr. James Boswell
of Auchinleck Advocat
Att Edinburgh

My Dearest
I had your sweet and edificing letter, which was a great
cordial to me. I had a letter from my Sister Mary in
answer to mine, she writs that she spock fully to
Ochiltrie concerning the contents of my letter, and
that he said ther is nothing he more desires then to
end with us, and that it shall be non of his fault if it
be not immediately done; and she bids me assure my
self that all that lays in her power to have matters
ended shall not be wanting, for that she is most
desireous to be at a point with us. So my Dearest I
would fain hope you will get all ended in time that you
may get the occation of the coach, for I should be
sory you missed so good an occation; I have sent you
My Dear hereinclosed a coppie of the paper my Sister
Mary gave me of what she obliged herself to furnish
me upon my questing what is therin named, and
likways nott of what I have already got of those
things, for perhaps both may be befor you can end,
and I am unwilling anything should retard you, seeing
the coach is to go soon.

My Dearest I confess it is not very easie to me to think upon your going so farr a journey[4] , especiall now when it draws near the time, but I submit, and pray that the Lord may graciously be pleased to preserve you from all hurt in your going and return, and that we may have a comfortable meeting againe if it be his holy will. I apprehend my Dearest you will not yet gone west with me befor you go, when I much long to be, but I desire chearfully to submit to the good providence of God in all things, who orders all well and wisely and knows better as we do what is fitt for us. I beg my Dear you may not trouble yourself to come here befor you can conveniantly do it. I shall give you no further trouble at this time. I pray that the sweet presence of God may ever accompany you, I am

Culross August i4   My Dearest
    1704   Yours most affectionately
                         Eli. Boswell

 be pleased my Dear when you writ to your Uncle to inclose this that I have written to him which I send you here inclosed

---

(4) My great grandfather's family history (detailed later) mentions an occasion when James went up to London on business connected with the sale of the estate of Lennox to the Duke of Hamilton. Possibly this was that occasion.

Chapter 1: Family History

Both Elizabeth and James were descended from ancient and distinguished Scottish families. Elizabeth's Bruce ancestry led back to Robert Bruce. Her grandfather Sir George Bruce of Carnock had been an ingenious entrepreneurial type, who had mined into the coal under the Firth of Forth through an artificial island, pumping the drainage water into salt pans, the resulting salt and the coal being sold in Scotland and on the Continent. Sir George's elder son Edward had been created Earl of Kincardine by Charles I, and on his death unmarried in 1662 the younger son Alexander became second Earl.

Alexander fled to the Continent in 1650, returning on the Restoration in 1660. During this decade, he lived in both Bremen and Holland. A possible explanation of his presence in Holland is given in the New Shell Guide to Scotland, 1978 : -

"----Cromwell defeated and executed Charles. He cared little that the axe he used for this purpose also beheaded the King of Scots. The Scots did. They were horrified, but saw an opportunity of resolving the conflict between loyalty and faith. They invited Charles's son and heir, later Charles II, to Scotland and crowned him on

5

condition he supported both covenants [pressing for Presbyterianism throughout the Kingdom].

This was too much for Cromwell. He invaded Scotland. The Scots invaded England, but were eventually defeated. Charles escaped from the island, and, until the Restoration of the Monarchy in 1660, Cromwell ruled over Scotland as well as England."

Bruce had presumably backed Charles, and in a Scotland under Cromwell would have been in a threatened position, so must have felt it prudent to follow Charles into exile.

After returning to London, Alexander then appears to have been on the founding Committee of the Royal Society in late 1660. Before returning to Scotland on his succession as Earl in 1662, he assisted Christiaan Huygens in unsuccessful attempts to use pendulum clocks to calculate the longitude, using his elder brother's ships on their trading voyages, though apparently an extremely poor sailor[5].

---

(5) From "The Invisible College" by Robert Lomas.

While in Holland he married, in 1659, Veronica van Aerssen van Sommelsdyck, youngest daughter of Corneille (Cornelius) van Aerssen van Sommelsdyck, Lord of Sommelsdyck and Spyck. We have a family paper apparently quoting from a "Letter from Lord Auchinleck to his son James" which states ; -

" You enquire --- about our Dutch relations --- I shall tell you what I know. The first of the family of Somelsdyke [Lord Auchinleck's spelling] was Francis --- the next person was Cornelius --- he was my Great Grandfather. He had one son who was murthered in a mutiny at Surinam, of which he was at one time Governour: and besides that son he had seven daughters, who got great fortune. Four of them were married, one to the Earl of Kincardine my Grandfather; her name was Veronica van Aerson van Somelsdyke. I have their contract of marriage in my possession, signed by the Earl and her and her father Cornelius. Cornelius married Lucia de Walta, whose two pictures are at Auchinleck".

PLATE 4 : VERONICA COUNTESS OF KINCARDINE
(née VAN SOMMELSDYCK)
(1633 – 1701)

PLATE 5 : ALEXANDER BRUCE
2ND EARL OF KINCARDINE
(1629 – 1680)

PLATE 6 : LUCIA VAN SOMMELSDYKE
(née DE WALTA)

PLATE 7 : CORNELIUS VAN AERSSEN
VAN SOMMELSDYCK

On his return to Scotland, Alexander became "a prominent statesman after the Restoration, made 10th July 1667 an extra Lord of Session, and one of The King's Commissioners for the Government of Scotland, but dismissed from The King's Councils by the influence of Lauderdale"[6]. His elder brother Edward, 1st Earl, died unmarried in 1662 and Alexander succeeded as 2nd Earl.

By his marriage with Veronica, Alexander had two sons, Charles Lord Bruce (probably the baby in the portrait of Countess Veronica), who sadly died unmarried in 1680, only a few months prior to the death of Alexander himself. The succession went to his younger brother, another Alexander, who also died unmarried in 1705. There were also three daughters, Mary, who married William Cochrane of Ochiltree in 1681, Anne, married Sir David Murray of Stanhope in 1684, and Elizabeth. On the death of her brother Lady Mary undertook a court case in the Court of Session against Sir Alexander Bruce of Broomhall in an unsuccessful attempt to claim the honours of the Earldom in her own right.

Prior to 1504, the Auchinleck estate had been in the possession of the family of Auchinleck of that Ilk. According to Dane Love ("The History of Auchinleck – Village and Parish", pp.16-24), the first of these was Nicol de Athelec, listed in the Ragman

(6) Information from Burke's Landed Gentry, 2001.

Roll (a list of Scots lairds who had, mostly under duress, submitted and sworn fealty to King Edward [I] of England between 1292 and 1297), who was apparently uncle to William Wallace, and fellow warrior with him at a battle in Glasgow, in which the Scots took the Castle from the English. The line ended with Sir John Auchinleck:-

> "---just what happened up to the arrival of the Boswells in 1504 is not fully known. Many accounts --- state that Sir John Auchinleck disponed[7] the estate to his eldest daughter without the consent of his superior, that is King James IV. Thus the barony 'recognosced', or was returned to its superior, who granted it to another, in this case Thomas Boswell, a younger son of the Boswells of Balmuto"

The Boswell history thus commences with Thomas, 1st of Auchinleck, who was killed with his King, James IV, at the battle of Flodden in 1513, together with his elder half-brother Sir Alexander Boswell, 3rd of Balmuto.

Family tradition tells that for services rendered to the Monarch Thomas had been awarded the right to supporters on his Coat of Arms : -

---

(7) *Scots law;* to make over to another, in legal form (Westminster English Dictionary)

"----And on a compartment below the shield --- are placed for supporters two greyhounds: proper, collared Sable, each collar charged with three cinquefoils Argent [the symbol for Boswell], and thereto affixed a leash passing the forelegs and reflexed over the back Gules" [8]

My great grandfather John Alexander Corrie Boswell (1835 - 1872) wrote a family history, which being compiled almost one hundred and fifty years nearer the period under discussion, contains much very useful and relevant information, and from which I quote : -

"David Boswell, son of James Boswell was born 1st January 1640 at Kepton in the Parish of New Cumnock. He lost his mother while very young which was the cause of his education being neglected, for she was a pious and prudent woman whereas his father took little care of him --- He was sent to the school of Cumnock and began Latin but made little progress, so that in his future at the college of Edinburgh he was deprived of much benefit he might have derived from the lectures".

---

(8) From the Extract of Matriculation issued to my grandfather Henry St. George Boswell by the Lyon Court in 1928.

PLATE 8 : DAVID BOSWELL, 6TH OF AUCHINLECK
(1640-1713)

PLATE 9 : ANNA BOSWELL
(née HAMILTON) (1640-1711)

Dane Love, p.41, states: -

" In 1672 [about the time of James senior's birth] David Boswell, 6th of Auchinleck, received notice of ratification of the lands of Auchinleck, with the exception of those disponed by himself to William, Earl of Dundonald, in liferent, to Dundonald's only son and to Sir John Cochrane of Ochiltree [father of William], in fee."

Could it be that this was the source of the debt that seems to have caused such problems between James and Elizabeth, and William. Certainly it must have created an awkward situation, with the sisterly relationship.

"In 1666 David Boswell married Anna daughter of James Hamilton of Dalzell, by Jean daughter of Sir John Henderson of Vordel, a lady of eminent piety with whom he lived happily. They were both extremely frugal and diligent managers, and strove hard to save the family from ruin.

On his Uncle's death [David Boswell, 5th of Auchinleck] David Boswell succeeded to Auchinleck in 1661 but found the estate much encumbered --- in all there were some 90,000 merks[9] of debt and liabilities besides the annuity of 3000 merks [to Margaret Stuart, his uncle's widow] and strove hard to save the family from ruin: [a habit James and Lady Elizabeth seem to have maintained] --- David Boswell had two sons and three daughters: -

♦   1st son, James his heir

---

(9) S.D.(J). gives the merk as "An ancient Scottish silver coin in value 13s and 4d of our money, or 13d and 1/3 Sterling (1846), so c. 70p, but obviously far more at present values. An appropriate multiplier seems to be approximately 70 - 100

- 2ⁿᵈ John who purchased Balmuto from Andrew Boswell and married 1726. His son was [later] Claud Lord Balmuto ---

- 1ˢᵗ daughter Jean married to John Campbell of Horsecleugh --- She died a year after her marriage leaving no heir.

- 2ⁿᵈ Margaret married to Captain Hugh Campbell a son of Sir Hugh Campbell, and left several children.

- 3ʳᵈ Anna married to George Campbell of Treesbank, a grandson of Sir Hugh Campbell of Cessnock, and left several children.

David Boswell was seized with a palsy a good many years before his death which affected his memory a good deal. His wife continued strong and vigorous till a short time before her death which occurred in 1711. She had all her life been remarkably devout and on her deathbed she called all the members of her family around her and gave them much proper and pious advice. After this she passed away with perfect composure.

David Boswell survived his wife two years and died in 1713 at the age of seventy three.

James Boswell elder son of David Boswell was born in 16--"

17

[The International Genealogical Index quotes 'about 1680', which seems highly improbable as it infers James passing Advocate at the age of eighteen; we have in our records an unauthenticated date of 1672 which is perhaps more acceptable. Craik states (James Boswell, The Scottish Perspective p.8) : - ' In the fashion of the time Lord Auchinleck studied Civil Law at Leyden and was called to the Bar in December 1729 ' ; i.e., at age 23. James passed Advocate in 1698 as we shall read, so would have been 26 if born 1672, which seems quite reasonable].

"He is represented as 'from his infancy virtuous and careful'. His father placed him at the school in Ochiltree, then of great reputation, Sir John Cochrane of Ochiltree having taken pains to provide a good Master, and to procure all encouragement for him so that most of the noblemen and gentlemen's sons were educated there. The Master's name was Mr. James Boig. He was an excellent scholar, and kept great authority in the school. James Boswell used to tell that at first he had an aversion to books, particularly to reading Latin, but his father conscious of what a loss he had himself sustained from the want of it joined with Mr. Boig's severity and forced him to read it. One day Mr. Boig had whipt him for want of his lesson, so he ran home and first made great complaints to his mother, who came and told his father who appeared much offended. Upon this the youth came in and made great lamentations to his father, who replied 'I shall be quits with Mr. Boig, for since he has whipt my son I shall whip his scholar', and accordingly whipped him again severely and sent him back to school. This had a happy effect, for after that he submitted to his master and made great proficiency.

Having become a complete Latin scholar he went on from the school of Ochiltree to the University of Glasgow. While there he had as a companion at his father's expense Allan Logan afterwards Minister at Culross, the family of Logan being then in reduced circumstances. Having finished his course at College James Boswell next went to Edinburgh and wrote [i.e., studied to become a Writer to the Signet, a Scottish solicitor] in Crawford of Crawfordjohn's Chamber till 1695 when being prompted by a desire to study the Civil law, he with great difficulty and chiefly through the interposition of Hamilton of Whitlaw one of the Senators of the College of Justice, obtained his father's consent to go over to Leyden to study. Accordingly he went there and stayed till 1698, when he returned to Edinburgh and passed Advocate to great applause. Lord Whitlaw who was his cousin on his mother's side was the greatest man at that time on the Bench and conceived a great fondness for him. Through this interest James Boswell first came to be noticed, and having got into some business before Lord Whitlaw died, his employment daily increased. He was in all the great cases where there were several lawyers and besides had a multitude of smaller causes, and many from peoples causes which he took up from charity"

At this point it is instructive to quote Craik, "James Boswell, The Scottish Perspective" [1994], p.7 :-

" The grandfather [he is discussing James the biographer], also James, was admitted as a member of the Faculty of Advocates in 1698. He is said to have had a large practice but appears to have been a bit of a plodder: so slow indeed, that he was said never to have understood a cause until he lost it three times. In his invaluable reminiscences of the time Ramsayof Ochtertyre describes the grandfather as a 'slow dull man of unwearied perseverance and immeasurable length in his speeches'. Be that as it may, at the time of his death in 1749, when James the younger was nine, he left the estate in financial good heart so as to enable both his son Alexander and his grandson to improve and profit by it".

[Can one detect Lady Elizabeth's frugal hand and mind at work here ?]

Also Pottle, "James Boswell, The Earlier Years", p.9 : -

"He was given to fretfulness, melancholy, and fear of his latter end; that he could make enemies is shown by the prayer of the old laird of Gilmillscroft [James Farquhar, and some three miles north - east of Auchinleck], who used in his family worship to petition the Almighty to pour down of his choicest curses on Mr. James Boswell of Auchinleck, advocate".

One wonders what terrible occurrence gave rise to this - could it have been one of the causes he had lost three times and still didn't understand ? Or, in view of the relative proximity of Auchinleck and Gilmillscroft, a possible territorial dispute in which Farquhar came second–best?

Again Craik pp. 2-3: -

" The practice of advocate in eighteenth century Scotland was geared to suit the requirements of its predominantly land-owning practitioners. The court terms were such as to allow the lawyer-landowners to attend to their estates in the crucial seasons of springtime and autumn. Even yet, the Scottish court 'vacations' reflect this pattern, although, for the busy practitioner, these have long ceased to be times when court work could be suspended".

While David Daiches also tells us in "James Boswell and his world", p.10, that

"the Court terms were from 12 June to 11 August and from 12 November to 11 March".

So it will be noted that the letters seem to date from the complementary periods of the year and also this is probably an explanation of how many of their themes are unresolved. Presumably they were brought to a conclusion during James' period on the estate during the court vacations.

Dane Love, p.52, tells us [James] "was reported by his son to have a 'melancholic turn', but was never troubled with this during session time, being devoted to his work. At the vacation he had so few hobbies that he suffered from depression". So he was probably what would today be called a "workaholic". And did James junior, who was well-known as a depressive, inherit the tendency from his grandfather?

Letters No. 3 to 7 (1708)

No. 3.

Auchinleck   4 June

My Very Dearest Sweet Heart   1708

I hope the bearer shall bring me a letter from My Dearest acquainting me with the good news of my Sweet Dearests safe arraivell which I long to hear. We are all here blessed be God as when you left us, but I think I have my health rather better, I have both my health and my stomach almost as well as ever so I beg My Dearest may be in no ways anxious about me. John Sedon came here yesterday he has made the Clocke go but he is to stay till tomorrow that he may see how it have altered the stance of it, we have sett it at the side wher the Candelier is, wher I think it stands much better, it is both more in the view, and stands much firmer, I doubt not the shacking of the door had a great influence upon its going so ofte wrong. I forgot to sett upon the memorandum a braid with the letters for Vetie My Dearest may send it with Slouen who goes in upon monday. I am to send some temmen[10] with him to Mrs Hamilton that she may be pleased to cause lift it for me, but I will direct it for My Dearest for Slouen knows not wher she lives, I shall writ to her and send My Dearest the letter also the Children I bless God are all well, but am still expecting they will [word missing under seal -? "take"]

---

(10) Temmen; as "Tammy" - "One of the basic fabrics of childrens' everyday wear in the seventeenth and early eighteenth centuries"; from "Clothes and the Child" by Anne Buck.

the missels, Jean Key has taken them, she went to her
Fathers yesterday, she laie with poor Davie that same
night they struck out but we knew not till the
morning, she was compleaning the day before that she
was not well but we thought it had been but a cold
however we see no sign of Davies taking them, I
never saw him blessed be God better every way, he
sleeped as well this night with Jean Templeton as ever
he use to do and cry'd not in the least, he truly is a
Sweet Child as ever I saw, Lord if it be his holy will
spaire him and make him his servant, I hope he shall
yet be a comfort and a help to his dear Papa.[11] That
same day My Dearest went away we catched the
?hiec[12] sparrow it came into the closet so we have
them both in the keag together and they eat very well
it is just such sparrow as I had so long, the children
are much taken up with them farewell My Dearest I
shall give My Dearest no further trouble at this time I
am

My Very Dearest Sweetheart
Yours most affectionately whyle
Eli: Boswell

---

(11) Sadly this was not to be; Davie appears to have died aged
between two and four- see later for more details. Jean Key and
Jean Templeton must have been maids or childrens' nurses.
(12) S.D.(J.) gives "hick" -to hiccup possibly resembling the alarm call of the
sparrow. "keag" not given but must= cage.

No.4.

To
Mr James Boswell of
Auchinleck Advocat
Att
Edinburgh

My Very Dearest Heart

Since my last to you I had two of My Dearests sweet
letters, And I received all of the things you mention to
have sent by Slouen, for all of which I return My
Dearest very many thanks but particularly for your
letter by Slouen which I was indeed much
strengthened edified and refreshed by; it was indeed a
seasonable letter, and blessed be the Lord I have since
found by experience much of what you writ. I desire
to bless the Lord who was graciously pleased to give
me the occation of approaching to him at his holy
table, tho most unworthy of such a preveledge, as I
minded myself while ther I was made to mind My
Dearest and our little Children, and I trust got that
new and Everlasting covinant seal'd to us, My Dearest
that is a sweet covinant let us fervently plead here
upon, for tho he has promised all yet for all these
things will he be sought for, that he may pouer out
upon us the spirit of prayer and supplication, and that
that may be what may be our chief concern that one
thing necessary, remembering that we are not our
owne being bought with a deir price indeed, not of
silver or gold but with the precious blood of the Son
of God; let us admire that infinit free love to us
sinners, it may indeed put us to a non plus to say with

the Psalmist what we shall render to the Lord.I hope
My Sweet Dearest as we have given up ourselves to
him we shall be made wholly to him, and that when
this short time shall be finished we shall glorify him
through all Eternity, he has prepared a place for us, let
him then have his aboad in our hearts, and let it be
still the Echo of our soul non but Christ, non but
Christ.   Mr Lourie designs to give the sacrement
some time in August, the Lord fitt and prepaire for it.
Poor Mr Lourie meet with a sade accident going to
Ocheltrie upon Saturday with design to preach, he fell
off his horse, and the horse fell above him and laie a
considerable space befor they could get him off, his
leg was hurt and his side so that he could not preach,
and was necessitat to go home in Watersyds[13] chais
which he did that same night and has not been able to
come out since and I hear is not preach upon
Sabath.My Lady Overkirk gives me an account in her
letter of My Lord Bellamonts death, he died three
weeks after he came to the Baiths, she writs was very
sensible before he died of his sinfull state and weept
bitterly, when death approaches it makes us see things
with a nother view. I am glad My Dearest has not
come for it would have been a great toill for you for
so short a stay, the time is now drawing fast on that I
hope I shall againe enjoy My Sweet Dearests most
desireable company for some time together, which
much do I long for. My Dearest befor you went from
here you was speaking that you designed to send some

---

(13) John Cochrane, William's younger brother.

horses to Lith for meal, I think My Dearest it wer very fitt you did it, for no doubt but you will have much advantage thereby, for we have frequent occasions of giving it out, and your Sister Madam Campbell I believe will need yet a good deal, and if we get no more provided she can get no more, other ways we will want for our own familie, so My Dearest will be pleased to let me know if I shall send the horses for that end. Sir Davids Sons are not come yet so that I am hopefull they will not come before My Dearest come alongst with them. My Dearest will be pleased to send two three pund kitshen sugar for it gos further than the loaf sugar for anything in the kitshen. Our new servant pleases me still better and better. She seeks nobody under her so I think it is needless for me to offer one, besides I think we but have too many servants I would fain be at keeping fewer. Veties gown fitts her very well it was a little too narrow but I have made let it out so it is now very well. My Lady your Mother desired me to writ to you that the stuff she sent in last week she will pay for the fitting of it herself, but she has now sent in some lineing to stamp[14] which she hopes you will pay, and so do I, if My Dearest can get it done. I bless God we are all here in our ordinary I was nothing the worse of the travel I made to and fro Ocheltrie, I am now wholly free of that trouble I had, I cannot yet judge what it was, or if I be so as you know it is but to much my desire to be, and therefore prehaps the Lord thinks

---

(14) Stamped Linen. Generic term for linen prestamped with designs. The Needlework Dictionary, Pamela Clabborn. 1976.

still fit to denay me therin, blessed be his holy name
who can do nothing amiss, and orders all things
wisely.

I shall give My Dearest no further trouble at this time
but pray God be with My Dearest and send us a
comfortable meeting in his good time. I am

My Very Dearest Sweet Heart

Auchinleck   Yours most affectionately whyle
3 July 1708   Eli: Boswell

[note at bottom of sheet : -]

 I forgot My Dearest to writ that My Lady Overkirk
gives her most affectionat service to you I give mine
to all friends as if named in particular. I believe the
letter I last wrot to My Lady Overkirk has been lost
for she makes no mention of it. I hope My Dearest
you will mind Allan Bounes bussiness poor man he
sent here a veal Mr Muir has sent the bill it is truly
extrodinary big for the age of it

No.5.

My Very Dearest Heart
I had your letter by Slouen, and all the things you
mention. I bless God you made so safe a journey to
Ed'r, and that My Dearest was in good health, which
is indeed most refreshing news to me. We are all at
present blessed be God in good health; little Sandie
has had the missels and was very sick for some days
but blessed be God he is very well recovered againe. I
was yesterday at Bawhary [15] wher I saw your Sister and
the Captain in good health and also little Hugh, it is
truly a sweet place, and a vast change upon the house
to the better since I was ther last, I took our little Vetie
with me who was very good company and mightiely
pleased she was with the journey, she grows every day
a pleasanter Child, Lord preserve her if it be his holy
will [16] and make her his servant and the rest of our
sweet little Children. The time is now drawing near
that I hope I shall againe enjoy My Sweet Dearests
most desireable company, which you may safely
believe I much long for. Lord send us a comfortable
meeting if it be his holy will. I have sent with the
bearer four pund of our Mains butter to Mrs
Craufoord, and two cheeses, the cheeses I believe will
be better if they wer older, I have sent also four brass

---

(15) Now Barquharrie, some two miles south of Auchinleck.
(16) He did. Vetie, or Veronica, grew up to become the wife of
   David Montgomerie of Lainshaw, and the mother of
   Margaret Montgomerie the first cousin and eventually the wife
   of James the biographer.

pans to change, but I desire but three back, which I
beg may be sent back with the bearer for we cannot
want them, after second consideration I have sent but
three pans for the other will serve yet for some time
ther needs but two be sent back one like the biggest
and one like the littlest, I have given the bearer a
harren pack for bringing me some hollands sand, I
would have about a six pence worth[17], be pleased also
to send ane unce blew for blewing linens. The bottle
of vinegar My Dearest sent last is not gone must have
a nother bottle befor Sir Davids Children come and
also a bottle of brandie, ther is no other thing I know
we shall need, I beg My Dearests pardone for
troubling you with so many things. If the temmen be
rady I hope My Dearest will be pleased to order the
sending it as also the stamped linen I sent to Mrs
Catherine Campbell to cause stamp. If Mrs Craufoord
can let me have our four kean chears I wish she would
send them, be pleased to let me know if I may writ to
her for them. I long to hear what is come of that
match of Charles Cochrane[18], and if ther be anything
done in Ocheltries bussiness with C: Areskine pray let
me know, and if Sir David Murray be in toun be

---

(17)harren, from "Hardyn; coarse; applied to cloth "[S.D.(J.)] ;
    and hollands sand, obviously a very fine-grained sand and
    used for cleaning pewter - so the Silvo or Goddards Plate
    Powder of the period.
(18)Second son of William, and Lady Mary, Elizabeth's sister,
    born 1683. The match appears to have come to nothing as
    Burke tells us Charles died unmarried in 1752.

pleased to give him my affectionat humble service
and to his son farewell My Sweet Dearest the Lord be
with you I am

My Very Dearest Sweet Heart

Auchinleck   Yours most affectionatelie

7 July 1708   Eli: Boswell

No.6.

My Very Dearest Sweet Heart
The inclosed was wrot to have been sent with George
Cochrane, but he was gone. [19] I wrot it in great heast I
know not if it be sense or non sense, however I have
sent it that My Dearest my see I did not writ when I
had occation. Since I received a nother from My Sweet
Dearest of the igth[eighth?] all I can say I am most
unworthy to receive such sweet affectionat letters but
I return My Dearest many thanks and I assure you
they are very refreshing cordialls to me more than I
can express. blessed be God that My Dearest is so well
recovered againe may you be long preserved if it be
the holy will of God. I bless God I am very well
againe I have been free this two days of that trouble I
wrot to you of, so that I designe God willing to
venture to go to Church tomorrow, I have thoughts of
going to Ocheltrie for the sacrement is to be given
there tomorrow eight days, and the Lord assisting I
hope to be there. My Dearest let me have the
assistance of your prayers, that I may be put in a
suitable fraim therefore, that I may be cloathed with
that weeding garment. as to my fraim, at present I find
much hardness and deadness, but I have no
complaints except against myself for my slothfulnes
and leasienesss, for I mind when I but make mints [20]
to draw near to him most rady is he to draw near to

---

(19)George Cochrane is not mentioned in Burke, but presumably
is some relation of William.
(20)mint- to insinuate or hint; or, to aim, to attempt S.D.(J).

me, yea often he prevents me and surprisingly shines his love in Christ upon my soul, which indeed is more valuable than all the world, and makes all things in the world seem but as loss and dung except in so farr as we teast his love in them, that love that passes all understanding, which will take ane eternity to prey into, and to praise him for so that we could begine that sweet song in time which will never be finished through all Eternity, when we shall cast our crowns at the Lambs feet, and when the thoughts hereof and the small teasts thereof is so sweet what must not the full fruition thereof be, when we shall free of these clogs of ours our bodys of sin and death, when we shall sin no more which now alas often makes such a sad separation betwixt our God and us. My Dearest writs that you have thoughts of coming home the beginning of the nixt month but My Dearest I am absolutely against it, for seeing your stay can be but two nights why should you toill yourself and be at so much expences for so short a stay, therefore I beg My Dearest that you may not come, for the thoughts of your toill would take away all the pleasure and satisfaction I would have in seeing My Dearest, and the time is drawing on fast when My Dearest I hope shall come and make a longer stay which indeed much do I long for I wish it could be so ordered that Sir Davids Children came not befor you come I have made fix the bed and have told Andrew Fisher to be diligent to put the Gardine in good order, we shall do all the best we can, I am the more easie in that we have got so perfect a servant as you have sent if she

33

continues as she has done hither we never had the like
of her, she does both her bussiness well and
pleasantly, I have no missing of Eppie Philp, so pray
do not engauge her back. Slouen brought every thing
you mention except the brandie and vinigar which he
said he could not get brought, the monteith[21]and
decanter are very pretty and setts off the candelier
extremely well with the new glasses you sent, it is now
as well provided as needs of all things I have sent back
Mrs Craufurds two codwars[22] I thought the first had
been sent back to her befor, it was a great fault that it
was so long keept I shall not feal [fail?] when I send
for flour againe to send some thing to put it in. My
Dearest needs send no more wengs [weags? unclear
here] [23] for they break in the carrieing, but if you think
Sir Davids Children will come here shortly ther must
be some white bread sent, and I think a pund of
bisketts, and ane unce of cinnamon.I cannot think
upon what more we will need. I think it is needless to
make Davie a new goun, I have made make him two
white frocks which when I was at London was as
much used for Children of his age as gouns with bib
and appron, My Dearest may be pleased to send him a
per or two of gloves little white muffells, pray order

---

(21)Monteith - "a silver bowl with a deeply notched rim - these
    bowls were originally intended for cooling wine glasses,
    suspended from the notches"Encyclopedia of Antiques, ed.
    Rosemary Klein, 1976.
(22)Codwar - pillow case S.D.(J.)but in this context being used as
    a container.
(23)Wengs / weags untraceable, but sounds like something edible
    and fragile.

that they bay [buy?] them large, for you know his hand
is pretty big, you may be pleased to bay Vetie allso one
per of the same sort. Davie must also have a per of
shoes those you sent last to Sandie fitted Davie exactly
so My Dearest may be pleased to send just such
another per and a per to Sandie almost also big for
ther is but little difference betwixt the bigness of their
feit, those that James Reed makes are so course that
they cannot well wear them when ther is strangers,
Vetie has a per of neat new ones already. I received
the two napkins and have keept one which I like very
well, the other I have sent back, which I have put in
Mrs Craufurds codwair, and a weastcoat and nightcap
of My Dearests, and two necks so that My Dearest
has now thertein [thirteen] necks.[24] I have sent the
window curtains for the orange room and drayen
[drawing?] room and the lineing for the cannope
chamber bed with the bearer for stamping, I have
writen to Mrs Catharine Campble and have desired
her to be pleased to cause stamp them, My Dearest
will be pleased to send her the letter, and bundle with
the curtains derected for her, and when it is done to
give her the mony for doing it, I am still putting My
Dearest to new expences and troubles, for all of
which I make no doubt My Sweet Dearest is very rady
to forgive me tho it wer much more.I wish Mrs
Hamilton would be pleased to make haste with the
temmen, and if it be rady to send it. My Lady your
Mother desired me to writ to you that she has sent in a

---

(24)Necks, and later gravats (cravats) and sleivs(sleeves ?),
    possibly part of the legal "uniform".

piece stuff to litt [25] which she hopes you will pay, I
believe it will not coast much so I hope My Dearest
will do it. I wonder much Ocheltrie can give you so
little, when he is owing you so much, I think My
Dearest should be free with him and tell him you
cannot lay out of it any longer, or ellse put to him to
give you a bond for thertie thousand merks and his
Son to corroborat it as you was saying, but I would
like much better you could get the mony that you
might pay off some principall soums which we are
now so vext paying the @rents[26] , and for the little
thing Ocheltrie has given I think if My Dearest thinks
fitt I would pay Mr Sanders Cunni[n?]gham with it, for
I suppose when he was here he was seeking his
principall soum, I am anxious to have him pay'd, so I
hope My Dearest will not break it for any other thing,
except it be some other debt more pressing to be
pay'd. [27] I just now received My Dearests letter you
sent with Logans Man he sent it with a nother Man
and sent me word any other thing he had he would
bring it monday so that I have not as yet got Veties
goun, I hope My Dearest continues well seeing you
writ nothing to the contrary.I was truly vext I was so
long without an occation to writ to you and the more
that I find My Sweet Dearest uneasie that you been so

---

(25)Litt - to dye S.D.(J.)
(26)Contraction for Annual Rent S.D.(J.).
(27)One gets the impression here that everyone was chasing
everyone else for money, and James' debt from Ocheltrie
seems an immense sum. We are told that the Darien Venture
some ten years previously had swallowed up half the capital in
Scotland. Was this sort of situation the unhappy aftermath ?

long without hearing from me, I am not worthy to be
so much minded by My Dearest, I wish the Lord may
make me a good wife to My Dearest I am sure I have
many tays therto. I see My Dearest has still a designe
of coming here, which makes me againe beg most
earnestly that you may not come, for as I said befor it
will be but toill My Dearest seeing your stay must be
so short, besides it will be very expencive which we
have need to shune considering how ill mony is to be
had but prehaps My Dearest forgets that when you are
a wheill at Ed'r, but truly the chief thing to be
considered and that which has the greatest weight with
me is the toill to your own person for I know My
Dearest does not agree with much riding. I shall do
my endeavour to get the cannope room plaister'd I
have sent againe and againe about lyme but ther is non
that has any rady neither will for a considerable time
so that I see no appearance that we will get the house
casten[28] this year for John Simmerall says it must be
twenty days sour'd befor he can make use of it for
casting the house, however when the lyme is rady it
may be laid in, and it will be the radier for the nixt
year, a house should be casten the beginning of the
year that it may have time to dray. The Children I bless
God are very well, little Davie has been troubled this
two three days with ane outbreaking in his face but

---

(28) Casten; to cast - to give a coat of lime or plaster ---
throwing it on with the trowel.S.D. (J.).

other ways blessed be God he is very well, and a
sweet little Man he is, he often speaks of his dear
Papa, and kest his hand to you just now when I but
named you and many a letter he writs to his dear
Papa.[29]now---

---

(29) We had always imagined "Papa" to be a Victorian
endearment; it is surprising to find it in use so much earlier.

No.7.

To
Mr James Boswell of
Auchinleck Advocat
At Mrs Craufurds Lodging
In Mills Squer in the Landmarkett
Att Edinburgh

---My Dearest I think it is almost time I wer giving
over, and to consider that My Dearest has some better
thing to be taken up with as to read my scribles but I
think I am a little to be excused since I have no other
way of converse with My Dearest tho my letters be
some what long and I am not afraid but My Sweet
Dearest will soon pardone me for that fault. I send
here a nother Summonds James Finle got farewell My
Dearest and send us a comfortable meeting in his
good time I hope My Dearest will not forget his poor
wife at the Throne of grace who shall ever be
My Sweet Dearest Heart

Auchinleck   Yours most affectionately
i9 June 1708   Eli: Boswell
[written across the fold] : -
My Dearest your Father remember you most
affectionately he is after his ordinary be pleased to
give my kind service to all as if named, particularly ---

[An incomplete fragment which seems to follow No.6]

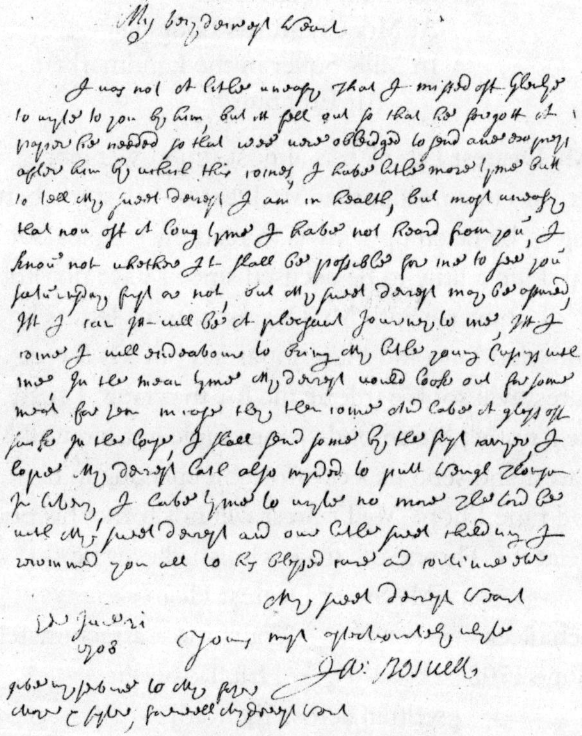

PLATE 10 : SOLE LETTER
IN JAMES' HANDWRITING

My Very Dearest Sweet Heart

The sole letter from James to Elizabeth: -

My Very Dearest Heart

I was not a little uneasy that I missed off ?Glenlye to
write to you by him, but it fell out so that he forgott
of ?paper that he needed so that [?I] was now
oblidged to send and was going after him by which
this comes, I have little more tyme butt to tell My
Dearest I am in health, but most uneasy that non off a
long tyme I have not heard from you, I know not
whether it shall be possible for me to see you on
Saturday night or not, but My Sweet Dearest may be
assured iff I can go will be a pleasant journey to me,
iff I come I will endeavour to bring my little young
Cusines with me. In the mean tyme My Dearest could
look out for some ?mead for them in case they then
come and have a glass of ?punch in the ?house, I shall
send some by the ?Ayr carryer, I hope My Dearest has
also mynded to ?pull/putt through ? - ? for ?library I
have tyme to wryte no more the Lord be with My
Sweet Dearest and our little sweet children I
recommend you all to his blessed name and continue
ever

My Sweet Dearest Heart

Edr June 2i   Yours most affectionately whyle
1708   Jas: Boswell

Give my services to my father and mother ,
farewell My Dearest Heart

41

The "young Cusines" mentioned are possibly the children of Sir David and Lady Anne Hamilton, Elizabeth's sister, though strictly speaking they would be James and Elizabeth's nephews. He was perhaps delivering them to their other aunt, Lady Mary, at Ochiltree, in view of the mention of their coming to the house.

CHAPTER 2: FAMILY MATTERS

An account of James and Elizabeth's family falls naturally into place at this point. Burkes Landed Gentry, The Kingdom in Scotland [19th Edition, 2001] and our family trees give Alexander (Sandie in the letters) born 1st April 1706, twins James and John (from the latter of whom I am descended), born 12th July 1710, and Veronica (Vetie in the letters) as the order of birth. However the letters make it clear that Veronica was the oldest. It appears that genealogists regard women as machines for producing the next generation of males, but are otherwise uninterested in their personal details, so we know little of these for Veronica. There is also David (Davie), seemingly older than Sandie. We have been able to trace David's Baptismal record as dating from 11th January 1706 (and Alexander's as 2nd March 1707), but none is traceable for Veronica, whom we suspect must have been born in 1705. The latest mention of Davie is on 29th July 1708, so sadly he must have died aged between two and four years, before the births of James and John on July 12th 1710, and probably during one of the Court vacations as mentioned by Craik and Daiches, so there is no further mention of him. As Lady Elizabeth herself says in Letter J3 to John in 1733, on the death of her sister-in-law's child "---poor woman it is havie upon her being the first breatch of her little flock, but bears it very Christianly " - as one could be certain she herself would have done in the earlier years of the century.

A note in Ryskamp and Pottle , "Boswell: The Ominous Years", p.164, helps to confirm, indirectly, the existence of Davie : -

> "In naming his children, Boswell [the biographer] followed the custom usual in Scotland with established families:first son named for father's father, second son for mother's father , third son for father's grandfather"

If we apply this to James and Elizabeth's family it works perfectly so far if we include Davie : -

- ◆ David - paternal grandfather = David 6th of Auchinleck

- ◆ Alexander - maternal grandfather =Alexander 2nd Earl of Kincardine

- ◆ James - paternal great grandfather = James, younger brother to David, 5th of Auchinleck

- ◆ John - here the system goes awry as his maternal great grandfather was Sir George Bruce of Carnock. Perhaps for some reason he was named instead after his uncle John, James' younger brother.

PLATE 11 : VERONICA BOSWELL (1705-?)

PLATE 12 : ALEXANDER BOSWELL 8TH OF
AUCHINLECK, LORD AUCHINLECK
(1707-1782)

PLATE 13 : JOHN BOSWELL MD (1710-1780)
IN PRESIDENTIAL ROBE OF WHAT LATER BECAME
THE ROYAL COLLEGE OF PHYSICIANS OF
EDINBURGH

Realization of the existence of Davie / David gives rise to the "What if---" syndrome - how would the Boswell family have been affected had he survived to reproduce ? David would have inherited the title and estate and become Boswell of Auchinleck on James' death in 1749; so Alexander, on becoming a Senator of the College of Justice would not have been able to call himself Lord Auchinleck and would have had to choose a different title; the "New House" as at present might not have been built, or at any rate probably not in its existing design; James junior could not have written his rather bumptious if not arrogant letter to Rousseau as it stands " Tell me is it possible for me yet to make myself a man? Tell me if I can be a worthy Scots laird. If I can - heavens, how much I fear the contrary !" And one could probably go further on this theme, culminating that it is extremely unlikely that the title Boswell of Auchinleck would have descended to myself !

Also, David, James' father, 6th of Auchinleck, as a result of the death of his infant grandson, was the last of the family to bear the name as a main name for almost three hundred years.

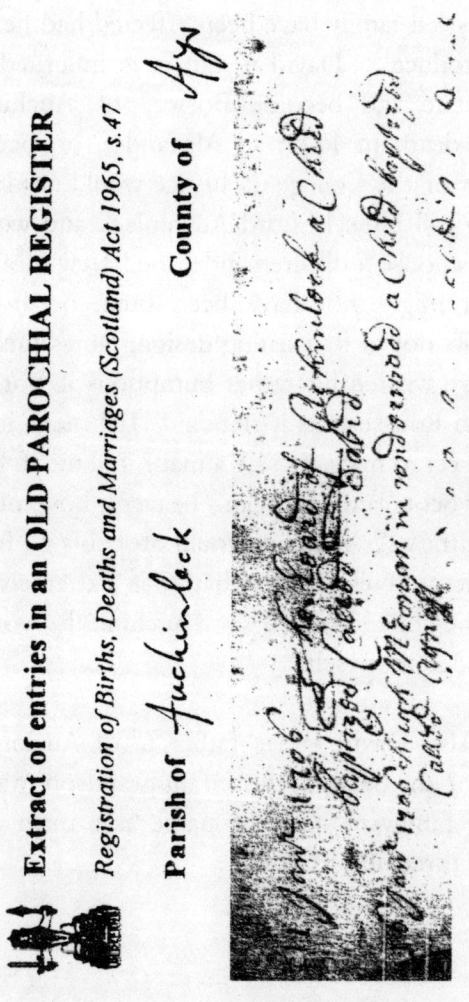

PLATE 14 : BAPTISMAL ENTRY OF PREVIOUSLY UNKNOWN SON DAVID

We had a similar realization, though on the scale of world history, a few years ago on a trip to Australia. We were taken to an Australian historical museum near Sydney where we learnt that as a very junior officer Napoleon Bonaparte had applied - and been rejected - to join an expedition, under the command of a Marquis de la Perouse, and shortly to set out to explore the western Pacific ocean, and which had sailed out of Australia's Botany Bay just as Admiral Philip's First Fleet landed there in 1788. Nothing more was heard of it till about twenty years ago when a ship's bell identified as coming from Perouse's ship was recovered from a wreck off the Solomon Islands some thousand miles north of Australia. It was said that King Louis XVI was so concerned that even on his way to execution he asked "and is there still no news of M. Perouse?" - so "What if --- ?". Bonaparte, had he been on the ill-fated ship, would not have survived either, and the whole course of history would thus have been rewritten.

Elizabeth and James' family seems to have had many health problems - coughs and colds of various types, including the "chinne-cough [could this be whooping-cough, or S.D.(J.) gives "chingily = gravelly"], the possibility of catching the "missels" - measles presumably, and both James and John had infections treated with a "Lochlitch", which S.D.(C.) tells us, though not quite with the same spelling, means a leech There is no mention of Elizabeth's having had to acquire one, so did households keep one in reserve for occasions of this kind, and if so, on what did one feed it ?

In the letter of 13th November 1710 Elizabeth writes specifically to acquaint James of her concerns about Jamie the elder twin's very large fontanelle[30], asking him to obtain advice from various Edinburgh doctors, including his uncle, his mother's brother Sir David Hamilton and also "Dos(s)intoun". [Sir David is mentioned in some family notes we have as being "the King's Physician", which I had imagined referred to King William III. However in the Dictionary of National Biography, 1890, we are told "He became a leading practitioner in midwifery, and was successively physician to Queen Anne, who knighted him, and to Caroline, Princess of Wales" (I am much indebted to Iain Milne, Librarian, Royal College of Physicians of Edinburgh for this information). So it seems the title must have been "The King's Physician" regardless of the gender of the monarch]. One of our family heirlooms is a gold and coral rattle, complete with whistle and bells, given by Sir David to John his great-nephew. And Elizabeth also obtained advice from the

---

(30)"Before birth the bones at the vertex and side of the skull are separated from each other by membranous intervals in which bone is deficient --- the fontanelles, so called from the pulsations of the brain, which are perceptible at the anterior fontanelle, and were likened to the rising of water in a fountain . The anterior fontanelle is the largest --- remaining open until the first or second year. --- Sometimes it remains open beyond two years , and is occasionally persistent throughout life.(Gray's Anatomy, 1877).

local doctor in Ayr, John Lockhart. Opinions seemed mixed, with one advising a "Plaister", another a "Pouder", and still others recommending "my applying nothing but what I have done already a scarlet cloth". James survived, to become a Writer to the Signet (a Scottish solicitor), apparently dying unmarried in c.1757, but it seems, having had mental problems - could these have been related to the large fontanelle ?

Even one of their horses had health problems (Letter No.16, 16th December 1710), for which Elizabeth was "thinking if she grows no better to send her to Glasgow to Swan, we shall neglect no means" We don't know who Swan was (the Veterinary Colleges of Glasgow and Edinburgh could find no record of him), but he must have been good for her to think of sending a sick animal some thirty miles for treatment. Again, unfortunately, we never learn the outcome.

Lady Elizabeth seems to have led a very frugal life, despite her descent from the Scottish and Dutch aristocracies. Probably, with the problems of capital already mentioned, she had no alternative. In Letter No.5, 3rd July 1708 she hints at cutting down on servants "our new servant pleases me still better and better. She seeks nobody under her so I think it is needless for me to offer one, besides I think we have but too many servants 1 would be fain at keeping fewer" Then in No.16, 9th December 1710, where James has apparently bought some new horse harness to go with their chaise, she tells him off for extravagance "--- and returns My Dearest many thanks but I am truly vext you should put yourself to so much expences on my account, I may say without a liee my mind is not set much upon those things, they are rather a burthen to me, I am sure the harness could not be cheap for they are very good ---". Again, she asks James to send bread from Edinburgh which seems strange for an agricultural estate "I intreat My Dearest may not send above one loaf, I have now wheat of our own which I am going to grind, and I hope it will make very good bread, and I think we may make our own product serve us [No.17 16th December 1710], and [undated fragment but almost certainly 19th July 1708] "--- if you think Sir Davids Children [This Sir David is probably Sir David Murray of Stanhope, the husband of Elizabeth's sister Anne] will come here shortly ther must be some white bread sent ---" . So it seems there were times in the year, or possibly it depended on the year's harvest, when their own flour ran out and they had to import bread from Edinburgh, but also she thought the imported bread from Edinburgh was more suitable for guests while "making do" with their own when it was just for the family. Letter No. 23 10th February 1711, is also telling on her viewpoint " I intreat you againe My Dearest send but one loaf, and send non with Murdock [the carrier] they coust you deir in baying, and they coust almost the half of their worth for carrage, one will abundantly serve for extrodinary strangers, and for others the flour we have will serve very well, and for sugar and rasins and those sort of things I get them as cheap and good at

Kilmarnock and they coust nothing for carrage".

J.A.C.Boswell gives an interesting and relevant quotation from Lord Auchinleck's journal : -

> " 'And I remember that although when my Father was in the country and company expected (which happened almost every day during his stay), there was always a very good dinner prepared: yet when he went away to Edinburgh, and so no company was expected, my Mother draped herself in very plain clothes, and we had commonly fleshless kail and eggs to dinner, pottage to breakfast; and bread and milk to supper --- At this time tea was not come in to be common, so that though my Mother always had it in the house, it was not used except when strangers came, and I can say that thus fed we all looked well and were in good health and spirits'. By this strict economy on the part of Lady Elizabeth James Boswell was able not only to clear off all the debts on the estate but also to make additions to the property".

"Ocheltrie" - William Cochrane, husband to Lady Mary, Lady Elizabeth's eldest sister seems to have been a perpetual problem to James and Elizabeth. Mary had married William in 1681, and at the time of the letters Elizabeth was obviously concerned over the state of their marriage. The huge debt he seemed to owe them, with apparently little effort to settle it, has already been discussed. Some ear-rings are mentioned but not in sufficient detail to uncover the facts – was he "selling off the family jewels"? Possibly to pay for drink – a John Donald is mentioned in connection with Cochrane. Was he a publican and was William Cochrane over-fond of the bottle? There seems a strong suspicion. In one letter there is mention of his being about to travel to France. Was this on business or to evade his debtors?

A brief note on the future history of James and Elizabeth's family can conclude this chapter.

David/Davie who died in infancy has been discussed earlier. Until studying these letters there had been no clue to his existence, but his presence falls neatly into place with the pattern of family naming given by Ryskamp and Pottle, though one can but wonder how previous historians did not question that Alexander, if first-born, did not fit the accepted Scottish custom.

Veronica/Vetie grew up to marry David Montgomerie of Lainshaw, and was the mother of Margaret who became James the biographer's wife by a first cousin marriage.

Alexander/Sandie is well known as the rather cantankerous and outspoken father of James the biographer, and as the possible designer, and builder, of the present Auchinleck house, now so spectacularly restored. Our son Robert was the last member of our family to visit the house in occupation, some forty years ago, and since then, as members of the Auchinleck Boswell Society, it has been with increasing depression over its state of decay and vandalism that we have paid our annual "pilgrimage" to view it, so all credit to the Landmark Trust who have carried out such a splendid restoration. Alexander died in 1782.

Little seems to be known of James/Jamie beyond his becoming a W.S. and his death in c. 1757.

John studied medicine in Edinburgh and in 1733 travelled to Leyden (see Letter J3) to study for his doctorate. We have his Doctoral thesis, "De Ambra" which is entirely in Latin. I did try to translate it some years ago from the relics of my schoolboy Latin, but found the medical Latin difficult and lost courage on it. I got as far as that it discusses ambergris, regurgitated by sperm whales, but what its medical uses were I never found out! In later life he became the Censor, or President, of the Edinburgh Medical Society which became later The Royal College of Physicians of Edinburgh, in which role we have a portrait of him, wearing his robes of office. He died in 1780.

LETTERS NO. 8 TO 10 (COMPLETING 1708)
No.8.

[An incomplete fragment]

To
Mr James Boswell of Auchinleck
Advocat At Mrs Craufurds
Lodging in Mills Squer in the
Landmarkett att Edr

--- My Dearest I had almost forgot to writ that My
Lady your Mother desired me againe to writ that she
hopes you will pay for the stamping of her linen so I
hope My Dearest will if you can conveniently. I have
here inclosed sent My D'st purss having forgot to give
it when My Dearest was here. Your Father remembers
himself most affectionately to you be pleased to give
my kind service to all friends as if named. I hear Mr
Lourie continues his resolution in giving the
Sacrement next month they say the second Sabath of
it Lord for Christs sake fitt and prepaire us therefore.
I hope your Brother has got a packett of papers of
Mr Henry Osburns I sent with Mr Fergisson at
Comlock[31]

[written on blank side of back in another hand] : -
    Auchinleck 19th
July 1708
Ldy E. Boswell

---

(31) Comlock;? = Cumnock.

No.9.

My Very Dearest Heart

I was much refreshed by your two letters by Slouen and James Murray to hear of the continuance of your well being, blessed be our good God. I am mightily pleased with the hopes of seeing My Dearest so soon, Lord send us a comfortable meeting if it be his holy will, which much do I long for. I shall be glad to see Sir Davids Children here, but the more since Mr Lourie has altered his resolution of giving the sacrement so soon, for at such ane occation devertions is not desireable, what time it will now be given is uncertain for Mr Lourie compleans much that he is not well ever since he got that fall, so that now he always sitts when he preaches, so till he grow better he cannot give it, but I hear it is to be given at the Soren[32] sabath come a fortnight. I received all the things My Dearest mentions by Slouen and returns My Dearest many thanks for minding so carefully all my triffels. Mrs Katharine Campbell writs to me the stamping of the linen for the bed and curtains coust 5 pence the elle[33] and ther is three and fortie ells of it which comes to just ten pund fifteen and six and a

---

(32)Soren; ? Sorn, some three miles north-east of Auchinleck.
(33)Elle; a measure of 37 inches but English elle = 45 inches S.D.(J.).

babi[34] for somme stamped calligo she sent me which makes in all eleven pund one shillen six pennies which I beg My Dearest may be pleased to pay her, I am still troubling My Dearest as for the temmen. I believe it would have been as best done at home, it will make me wiser a nother time, they say for a Scots proverb witt bought is worth two for nought and I hope it shall be so for me. I have sent with the bearer the three Bonds My Dearest wrot for and have rolled them in some stuff of your Sisters and have put all in the clog bag[35] so that I hope all will be safe. I wish My Dearest may get ended with Ocheltrie and his Son to your satisfaction, ther is nothing like hading [36] at them and being very brisk, which I intreat My Dearest you may. as for the hunder pound I am glad My Dearest is to get it that so you may pay off some of your pressing debts, it is a pleasant thing to pay principal soums, it takes off so many a rents, I hope My dearest will be persuaded to imploy Davids gould for that end also, I am sure if it please God to spaire him he will give you more thanks when he comes to be a Man for having so imploy'd it as if you should keep it by you. We have great want of Holland sand I intreat My Dearest you may be pleased to cause put up if it were

---

(34)Babi; Bawbee a halfpenny S.D.(J.) "This word is broad Scots for 'baby' the familiar name for the copper coins that came from the Mint during the infancy of Mary Queen of Scots, with the baby Queen's head on the face of each".

(35)Clogbag; saddlebag S.D.(C.).

(36)Hading; S.D.(J.) gives "had" as " took, taken, or carried", so here in the sense of "carrying on at", perhaps.

but a chopine [37] in the clog bag for the peuther has great need to be scour and any other sand but spoills it. The two loafs I am keeping them against Sir Davids Sons come but I am affraid they will not keep without mouling till they go away so that I think it will be fitt to send a nother if you can get occation, and a nother pund of bisketts, for I saw they loved them I gave them a good many when they went their way so that I have but few. I know no other thing we will need. I shall endeavour to provide the best meat this countrie can affourd I would gladly have had a stott to kill but Hugh Murdoch tells me he knows of non good. I shall give My Dearest no further trouble at this time hoping so soon to have My Sweet Dearest here the very thoughts thereof lifts up my heart for indeed My Dearest much do I long for you Lord send you a good journey and a comfortable meeting with us if it be his holy will I am

My Very Dearest Sweet Heart

Auchinleck   Yours most affectionately whyle

29 July 1708   Eli.Boswell

[enclosed in folded paper addressed] : -

To

Mr James Boswell of

Auchinleck Advocat

att Edinburgh

---

(37)Chopine; untraceable but obviously a small measure.

No.10.

My Very Dearest Sweet Heart
I was much refreshed to hear you had so safe a
journey to Ed'r, and that you was in good health,
blessed be our good God, long be it so if it be his
holy will. I received all what My Dearest mentions,
and returns you many thanks, the Children were much
pleased with their rasins, and returns their dear Papa
many thanks. I bless God we are all in our ordinary,
but we have great missing of you especially your poor
Wife, but I desire to submit to his holy and blessed
will who orders all well, and knows better than we do
what is fitt for us; in this world we must not expect
every thing we desire, it will make heaven the sweeter
the more crosses we have here, I trust My Dearest we
shall once meet wher we shall never part. I am glad
you sent a letter to the Moderator in favour of Mr
James Lourie being Minister here, you have extreamly
pleased many ther by, and truly I hope we may be very
well with him, I am persuaded we would never have
got any that would have got such unannimuss a call,
and to have had the place vacant for any time was not
desireable on many accounts, I hear Sir John Cochrane
is rageing that he is not own'd therin, and that he says
he will put a straw in the way, but we think it will be
but a straw which will soon be stept over. I wish My
Dearest now that My Lord Loudon is at Ed'r you
would see to get a right to the patronage from him, I
am truly more desirous then I can say that you may
have it, therefore I intrit you may use your endeavour

to get it, we may come to think it more valuable after this, I againe intreat you My Dearest do not neglect to seek it, I cannot think My Lord will be so ungenerous to refuse it , considering what your familie has suffer'd by him. I have your letter to Mr Campbell just now returned, he being gone to Ed'r but I will put a nother cover about it, and cause back it to the moderator of the Presbitery of Aire, and cause the Clark to deliver it to him, for we know not yet who will be moderator, I am afraid it will be worse for the bussiness that Mr Campbell is absent, but we will endeavour to have it as well as managed as we can, and I pray God so order in it as maybe most for his glory and the good of souls. David Thomson was with me desiring to know what you will do with him, he is much inclined to go back againe to Gibson, which by William Portess tack[38] he may when you will, I caus'd speak to John Thomson if he would take the other half of Langlands, but he declined it, I believe William Templeton in Longholme will take it providing it lay lie[39] this year, it being so extreamly run out, and so he will take it, as he has the Longholme a Whitsondays tack, they perswade me it will be no loss to you to let it lay lie ther being seven riggs[40] of mucked land which will be near two ackers, but I will do nothing till My Dearest give me your positive answer, which I intreat you may do by the

---

(38) Tack : A lease ; (S.D.(J.).

(39) S.D.(J.) gives Lye:"Pasture land about to be tilled", so presumably to lie fallow.

(40) Not traceable but must be an area of quarter of an acre from the context.

bearer, as also what you will do about the Dipleburn, Jannet Aird positively refuses to leave it, unless you put her out, for she says she is now well planished, and the mealen in good condition, so that she is able to pay her rent and also hopes to pay bygons piece and piece, John Baird positively refuses to take any part thereof with her, or with any other if Jannet be not satisfied to leave it with good will, Jannet says if you please she will get a Married Man that will take a pleugh tack with her, or ellse Jean Tennants Brother John Tennant will take a fourth part thereof as Hugh Baird had at first, John is they say very well able therefore, and is very well satisfied he being at the time free, I believe My Dearest knows him a very honest sort of Man, he is indeed beginning to wear up in years: I intreat My Dearest you may not feall to let me know your pleasure about it, I wish indeed methods could be lighted upon that Hugh Baird and Jannet could be separat, considering what is talked of them, John Baird told me his Brother is very well satisfied to leave the place, it is true he is a good tennant and I know not wher ellse you can put him, for the Longlands his Brother John positively refused it, and I believe he will not be inclined therefore neither, and no doubt it will lay very conveniently for William Templeton provideing you and he agree, he is very desirous to have matters adjusted betwixt you and him as to his fathers old rests, and to take a new tack, for he designs to marrie but that must be refer'd till you come home. I sent Mr Roger a years arent the day after you went from this, I thought you

told me you pay'd him a year at Ed'r but I could not
find any discharge from ther, the last discharge was
for a years arent you sent him last year just befor you
went to Ed'r preceeding Wh: [? Whitsun] 1707, so
this I have now got is only pre: Wh: 1708, for he said
he got non from you at Ed'r, prehaps I am in a
mistake that you told me. My Dearest will know. I
have also sent Netherplace two years arent so he is
now pay'd preceeding Wh: 1708. John Good was with
me I told him I should give him a Precept when he
brought me his discharge which he promised to bring.
I have sent with the bearer four ston of butter
according to your orders two ston to Mrs Craufurd
and two to Mrs Hamilton your Cusine, I have also
sent Mr Hugh Campbells cheese to Mrs Craufurd.
receive your white coat and vest, and two shirts, five
necks, four gravats, one per of sleivs, one slip for your
nightcap, you will be pleased to send me the double of
the inventar of the linens you took with you for I have
forgot what I sent, so I cannot be sure if I want any
more of your linens, I shall send your other two new
shirts nixt time Slouen goes for now they are not rady
you may send any durtie linens you have and I shall
take care to send them back clean, I beg My Dearest
may send me Holland for making you necks and
sleivs, I hope you will not forget to make yourself a
hansome nightgoun and let me know by your first that
you have done it. you will be pleased to send me with
the bearer five dosen of bras rings for the tour de litt,
and some holland sand, I have sent a poch for puting

it in, be pleased also to send a firican[41] of sop, no more we stand in need of, if it be not some white bread, so I intreat you may send no other thing ---

[This letter is incomplete, but from the context of the Whitsun (May) dates it must be post-Whitsun 1708, possibly during the autumn Court session].

---

(41)? firkin, for which Westminster English Dictionary gives " a dry measure used in Scotland, of 35 pounds".

Chapter 3 :

Lady Elizabeth, the Kirk, and Religion.

It is clear from even a very superficial reading of the letters that both James and Elizabeth were extremely devout. Indeed in one or two of the letters she gets quite carried away, and we have almost a full blown sermon! It seems some of her Sommelsdyck aunts, sisters to Countess Veronica, belonged to a sect called Labadists - ["La Badie, Jean de (1610 - 1674) French divine, founder of the school known as the Labadists --- his ideas --- included community of goods within the church, the continuance of prophecy, the sanctity of marriage between two believers, the continuous Sabbath, etc. --- (which) brought them into frequent collision with their neighbours and with the magistrates"- Encyclopedia Brittanica]. So it seems probable that Elizabeth must have had some of this passed on to her on her visits to Holland. J.A.C.Boswell also informs us that : -

"Lady Elizabeth had been educated as an Episcopalian and entertained a great friendship for Mr. James Aird Minister at Torrieburn [c.3 miles east of Culross on the Fife coast] and for Mr. George Munro Minister at Dollar both Episcopalians and who corresponded with her. She was led to become a Presbyterian chiefly from conversing with Mr. G. Mair, Minister at

Culross, who married her to Mr. James
Boswell.

James Boswell and Lady Elizabeth lived
in the greatest love till her death and in their
letters from 1704 to 1739 ---"

[This batch covers only the period from 1704 to
1711. Where are the remainder? They deserve
publication equally with these]

"---there appears a constant strain of
piety and resignation to the will of God, and
at the same time equal love and affection at
the last as at their marriage. 'It was a thing
truly extraordinary' says Lord Auchinleck
'that a Lady of quality who had been
accustomed to live in a very expensive
manner and had been a good time at
London and in Holland with the Countess
her Mother, should have put up with so small
matters, and so great retirement with perfect
contentment. But she was a lady of excellent
sense, a woman of religion. She knew it was
her duty to provide for her family, and
knew when to spend and when to spare; ---
all therefore was economy. And she never
wearied when alone, as she read a great
many books of Divinity, of which she had a
good collection, English, French, and
Dutch, several of which we have still' "

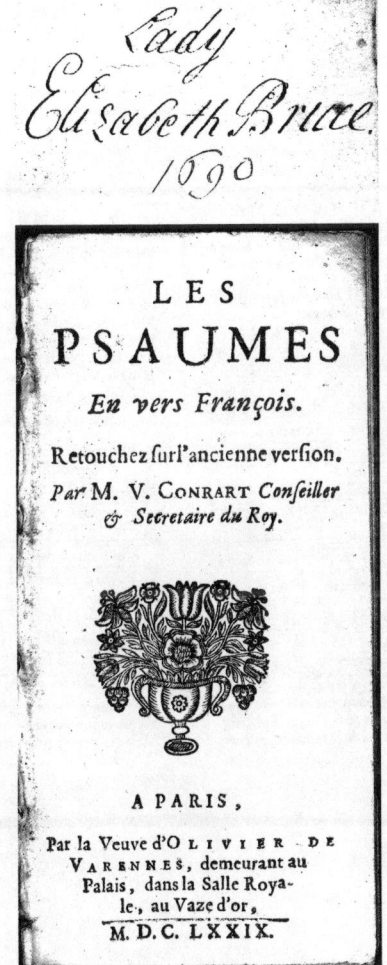

PLATE 15 : LADY ELIZABETH'S PRAYER BOOK
TITLE PAGE AND SIGNATURE

PLATE 16: PSALM 23

Dr. John must have inherited her Psalter, signed by her, in French, and with accompanying musical notation. One cannot help but wonder, though, however she had time for reading, with not only her family and estate duties but with her constant letter writing. Again J.A.C.Boswell quoting Lord Auchinleck:-

> " 'And it was this her principle made her put up most agreeably and contentedly not only with the small estate, but live in the greatest harmony with my Grandfather and Grandmother my two Aunts and My Uncle Balmuto who all lived in family for several years at Auchinleck after her marriage and Balmuto my Fathers only Brother till his marriage in 1726' ".

One factor that seems to have occupied Lady Elizabeth's mind considerably was the question of the Ministerial succession. We learn in Letter No. 5, 3rd July 1708, that the Minister, Mr Lourie, has had a fall from, and then been rolled on by, his horse, so is unable to preach the next Sabbath. He possibly suffered either a fractured femur and/or pelvis. Then three weeks later we learn " --- for Mr Lourie compleans much that he is not well since he got that fall, so that now he always sitts when he preaches --- ". The next we hear of the situation is in Letter No. 12, of uncertain date, but probably late 1710 : -

> " --- I am glad you sent a letter to the
> Moderator [of the Presbytery in Ayr] in
> favour of Mr James Lourie being Minister
> here, you have pleased many ther by, and
> truly I hope we may be very well with him, I
> am persuaded we would never have got any
> that would have got such unanimous a call
> --- "

Mr James Lourie must be the son of the old boy,
who has obviously died (but whether of his injuries we
never learn). He seems to be torn equally between
Auchinleck and "Kirkmighell", and various other
names are brought forward as potential candidates for
the succession. There is Mr Allan Logan of whom we
have learned from J.A.C.Boswell that David Boswell
paid for his fees at Glasgow University so that he
could be a companion for James, so obviously a great
friend. It appears however he was later "called" to be
the Minister at Culross. Also suggested are a Mr
Robert Willocks from Edinburgh, and a Mr Lang in
Craufurdjohn, but nothing more is heard of them.

There is also much talk of writing to the
"Presbitery" in Ayr, in connection with the ministerial
succession, Elizabeth does so and has to nag James to
do so himself and we finally learn that he has done so.

A quotation which well shows Lady Elizabeth's

caring side relates to the Minister's widow : -

> "My Dearest will be pleased to let me know what shall be done with the Ministers Gleib, if it shall be left, I think Mrs Lourie may be allow'd to stay in the house, till we get a Minister, for she will keep it right, besyds it will be a kindness done to her which she deserv's very well, both upon her own account and her worthie husbands".

The Register or List of Ministers known as Fasti Ecclesiae Scoticanae helps to fill in gaps in Lady Elizabeth's letters.

Mr James Lourie was called to Kirkmichael on 9th November 1710. His apparent doubts about the choice between Auchinleck and Kirkmichael may have been that he did not want, or think it appropriate, to follow in his father's footsteps or possibly the Presbytery advised him against it. He appears to have died, still in office at Kirkmichael, in 1764.

Mr. Lourie's, (or Laurie) successor at Auchinleck was John Grant, who does not appear to have been as conscientious as he should. We are told : -

> "John Grant --- admitted [to Auchinleck] 9th July 1712. He was accused at the Presb. 28th April 1731, of having been absent from his parish from Oct. 1729, and

providing an assistant for one month only, that he had visited the families in the parish only once in four years, and had dispensed the Communion not more than two or three times since his admission. His demission was accepted 9th June 1731; retired to London, where he became minister of a Presbyterian meeting house. On the death of his brother-in-law, Colin Campbell, the celebrated architect, he inherited a large fortune".

With her obvious piety and strong sense of duty one feels certain that Lady Elizabeth would have had some fairly choice comments in her letters over the next twenty or so years over Mr. Grant's indolent behaviour.. Indeed how was it he was tolerated for so long in the Parish? Was it Christian charity, and the hope, obviously vain, that his behaviour might improve, or could he not be removed from office for some ecclesiastical legal reason?

And she is trying to persuade James to write to Lord Loudoun to try to obtain the Patronage of the Parish (Letter No. 12, date uncertain, probably 1710 or -11) ; but it seems there was some disagreement between the Boswell family and Lord Loudoun in the past which gives rise to doubt : -

" I wish My Dearest now that My Lord Loudoun is at Ed'r you would see to get a right to the patronage from him, I am truly more desireous then I can say that you may have it, therefore I intreat you may use your endeavour to get it , we may come to think it more valuable after this, I againe intreat you My Dearest do not neglect to seek it, I cannot think My Lord will be so ungennerous to refuse it, considering what your family has suffered by him".

J.A.C.Boswell has something to say which may be relevant to this situation. Discussing the great burden of debt which David Boswell 6th of Auchinleck inherited on his uncle's (also David) death in 1661, he states: -

"--- Further on the occasion of Dame Margaret Hume's marriage to one of the Lords of Loudoun, when she resigned her life rent for an annuity of 2700 merks per annum which the Earl bound himself to pay her, the late David Boswell 5th of Auchinleck plus other gentlemen had consented to be [?] Cautioners or Securities for the Earl. Afterwards Loudoun being conveyed to his son [?who] did not represent his father and the Securities became responsible for the debt, and after his Uncle's death David Boswell had to pay at least 17000 merks on this score."

Slightly unclear but obviously the later

generations of Boswells felt a great resentment about the situation. The letters never tell us whether or not James bearded the lion in his den, and managed to obtain the Patronage.

However Dane Love , p.31, states : -

"After the reformation the patronage of the churches in Scotland was transferred to secular persons --- John, 1st Lord Loudoun, seems to have obtained the patronage of Auchinleck Kirk in March 1620 ---the kirk lands passed through a series of owners [till 1698]--- Soon after this the patronage was acquired by the Boswells, in whose hands it remained till patronage was abolished in 1874".

It seems strange there should be a more than ten year gap between the dates but could this be the episode initiated, or encouraged, by Lady Elizabeth in 1710-11?

Letters No. 11 to 18 (1710)

No.11.

--- I am sure I have wearied My Dearest by my long
scribles but I cannot get it helped when I writ to you
so I hope you will pardon me. I have sent a dosen of
yearon [yarn] seeing My Dearest will have me make to
some damask that you may be pleased to cause show
it to the weaver that he may let me know how much it
will take thereof for the elle waft, and how much for
the warp I would have it three quarters and a half
broad [interesting arithmetic here] I would also know
if I shall wash the yearon my self and wind it or if he
desires rarther to do it for I am informed at Ed'r the
weavers is not satisfied when they get not the yearon
to guide themselves. I beg pardon for troubling you
with so many triffles. Captain Hamilton is here yet he
has granted to stay till thursday but I cannot prevaile
with him to stay longer, I think your Cusine Mrs
Hamilton [possibly daughter - in - law to Sir David
Hamilton, James' uncle] will be the best you can
imploy about the damask or Margaret Kerr.

Now farewell My Dearest the Lord be with you and
send us a comfortable meeting if it be his holy will the
Children gives their humble duty to their dear Papa
they are all, blessed be God very well the little twinnes
are fine little Kairles[42]

         I am

                My Very Dearest Sweet Heart
Auchinleck   Yours most affectionately whyle
11 November 1710   Elizabeth Boswell

Be pleased to give my kind service to your brother and
to all his friends as named ther is to be sent a shirt and
a gravat of Mr Shaws

---

(42) As "Carl" - a man, or "Carlie" a little man; S.D.(J.). James
and John were born on 12th July ,so were five months old by
now.

No.12.

My Dearest
After I had sent away my letter to you I was finding
our little James Head. I was surprised to find such ane
open I never found the like any head that ever I found
not only above but alalongs down and at the syds of
his head I wish My Dearest you would writ to Sir
David Hamilton about it if he advises to applay any
thing upon it some is for my applying a strengthen
plaister and others are for my applying nothing but
what I have done already a scarlet cloth[43] I will do no
more till I have Sir Davids advice we may have peace
when we use means the child blessed be God is very
well now but they say all the hazerd is after they are
wean'd you may also be pleased to ask Dosintouns
advice some says ther is hazerd in delaying and the
sooner we use means the better you will be pleased
also writ the age of the child Adiow My Sweet
Dearest the Lord be with you I have sent five old
spoons to change

To

13 Nov'r 1710   Mr James Boswell of
Auchinleck Advocat

Att

Edinburgh

[in another hand on blank back]

Lady E. Boswell 13th November 1710

---

(43)Did the cloth's colour have any significance in eighteenth
century medicine ? And the Dosintoun mentioned is not
traceable.

No.13.

My Very Dearest Heart
I had yours by Slouen, and another by Samson and all
what you mention to have sent, I return My Dearest
heartie thanks for your mindfullness of me in letting
me hear so frequently from you, which is most
refreshing. I desire to bless God for the continuance
of your well being, and prays if it be his holy will that
it may long be so. The Children have all been very
distrest with the cold, except Vetie, but blessed be
God they are better, only John has it still very ill, he
has a very great cough I am afraid it will turn to the
chinne-cough, your Father and Uncle has also the cold
very ill, it is such seveur weather that few wants it but
I bless God I have not had anything of it yet, and
have had my health very well, only this day I have
been indisposed with a pain in my head which I hope
will soon go over. I am very glad to hear Ocheltrie is
come home, pray let me know what is doing in his
bussiness with C. Areskine, and how he carries to my
Sister. I am glad Mr Muir is like to be settled at
Closeburn, I am afraid we get not Mr James Lourie to
this place, he has got a very unannimuss call both to
this place and Kirkmighell, against nixt Presbitery day
he is to give us his ansuer which he accepts of, he was
here, I find some has been endeavouring to discourage
him in his coming here, and chiefly by making him
believe that you have no kindness to him, wherefore I
beg earnestly My Dearest you may writ a kind letter to
him, that he may be undeseav'd thereof, for I believe if

he had all encouragement imaginable if he thought he
had not your kindness he would not come, I hope if
the Lord so order in his providence that we get him
we will be very happie with him, but I am much afraid
we get him not, therefore I entreat you may writ the
more earnest to him, let my letter be the shorter that
you may have the more time to writ to him, which I
again earnestly beg you may do. as for my writing to
my Nephew Mr Murrays Lady, I have been so long
without writing that I know not how to begine, so I
think you must be pleased to make my appologie to
her, and give her my humble service, other ways My
Dearest will be pleased to writ me a scroll at your own
convenientie what I should writ which will much
oblidge me. Andrew Bruce tells me that his brother is
now satisfied to come here for the wage you offer'd
for he is come from the service he was in, Andrew has
written a letter to him that if you be satisfied to take
him you may be pleased to send the letter to him.
Andrew is not very well pleased with John Dalrymples
work, yet he thinks he is as good as any you will get
here away that is not accustomed to that sort of work,
so if My Dearest thinks fitt we may keep John
Dalrymple till pleugh time, for ther will be work
enough for all three, considering what is to trench and
young trees to transplant, and to bring any upon days
wages it would soon run up to a great fiee. Andrew
desires to know if you will have your Nurserie at the
side of the avenew wher you design'd. the Lycks are
not yet ended, but they are bussie about them. As for

levelling of the green all is of oppinion that the pend[44] should first be made, because it will take a vast deall of earth to lay upon it so what wil be taken off to leavell the green may be made use of for that effect, My Dearest will therefore be pleased to let me know if I shall cause make the pend or not. John Lockhart in Air was seeing us, I shew'd him our Jamies head, he says he has seen many such, and worse, and yet become very fine Children, but he makes them always applay a plaister of Mastick and other things proper for the head, which plaister he makes just as large as the open of the head is, he says he has seen it have very good effect, and he has applay'd upon Children of a month old, he told me all the Children he has alive ther heads were as open as Jamies, but he applayed plaisters upon them all: I shew'd him Dossintouns derection, he does not much approve of the pouder, he does not think it will have much effect upon Jamie, he thinks it is good for strengthening the head and keeping the head right when it is right, so that he advised to make use of it for Johne, but said ther was a necessity to make use of a plaister to Jamie, he is persuaded if Dossintoun saw the Child he would advise the same, but it is hard to advise at such a distance, if My Dearest thinks fitt you may speak to Dossintoun about the plaister, John Lockhart is to send me a plaister, but I will not applay it till I hear Dossintouns advice, the plaister is never to be taken off at the syde but as the head closes so much to be

---

(44)Pend; S.D.(C.) gives "block of sandstone; arched roof vault or canopy; lean-to; penthouse"; while S.D.(J.) gives "an arch".

taken off at the syde till it be queit close; the Child has
all good symptoms for he rests very well, and scours
well, runs at the nose, slavers and vomits a great deall,
and is the merriest Child as can be, and you know
thraivs very well for he is half as big againe as his
Brother.I intreat My Dearest you may not forget to
send me the Holland for making your linens, and
please send me one unce of threed at 8d the unce and
four drop of good shewing black silk, and one unce
blew for blewing the linens, and some Holland sand, I
am always troubling My Dearest with commissions,
and long scribles I am afraid I abuse your goodness,
considering how you are hurried with bussiness. But I
hope My Dearest will pardon me. I shall trouble you
no further at this time, I pray God be with you and in
his own time send us a comfortable meeting I am
          My Very Dearest Sweet Heart
Auchinleck   Yours most affectionatly whyle I live
    25 Nov'r   Elizabeth Boswell
     1710

Be pleased to give my humble and kind service to all
friends. I will writ to my sister and Lady Charles nixt
occation for now I cannot
           [on back] : -
26 Nov'r, My Dearest least you should be anxious for
my having written that I was indisposed with a sore
head yesterday I thought I would let you know that
blessed be God I am this day much better

No. 14.

My Very Dearest Sweet Heart
I had your most sweet affectionat letter dated the 23
of the last month for which I return you my most
heartie thanks. But I must quarle you for thinking that
any bussiness of My Dearests should be uneasie to
me, believe me My Dearest the only thing that is
uneasie to me therin, is that I have not that capacity
to go about them as I have inclination, otherwise if I
had ten times more of your bussiness it would be my
great pleasure to think that I could be any ways useful
to My Dearest in bearing further with you, which now
it is truly many times my grief that My Sweet Dearest
gets the burthen so much to bear alone, except as to
sympathie which I must own I have a great deal. As
for My Dearest not answering some times so fully my
letters, I wer unjust and ingrate to put any bad
construction upon it, I have so much experience and
am so persuaded of My Dearests undeserved
affection to me that tho you should writ non at all it
would be impossible for me to put any bad
construction upon it, so that I intreat My Dearest may
never straiten your self at any time under that
apprehension, for tho I must say your letters are great
cordialls to me, yet I desire not to buy them at the rait,
to be in any ways straitning to you when you so much
hurried with bussiness. My Dearest writs about my
coming to Edinburgh, My Dearest may easily believe I
want not aboundant of inclination, since my greatest
comfort in time is ther, but we must not always follow

our inclination, I think I may be more usefull to My
Dearest here, besides the poor Children would have
missing of me, as also your honest father, who is
pleased to shew a great reguaird for me, and he is very
craise,[45] I doubt not it would be a great adition to both
your trouble and mine if any thing should aile him if I
wer from him, so I hope My Sweet Dearest will excuse
me if I come not, but as for your coming here befor
the session be ended, I most earnestly beseech you for
the Lords sake you may not come, if you knew the
fear I am in about it I am sure My Dearest that you
would put me out of that fear, by writing to me
positively that you will not come, so let me intreat you
againe to satisfie me so farr to give me your promice
(unless any of us be ill that you be written for) that
you will not come, every body says you will kill your
self by your winter journeys, so I earnestly beg againe
you may give me no more occation for saying so.

---

(45) At first thought this was from "crazy" related to the stroke
we are told he had had, but S.D.(J.) gives "Craize" to creak, so
possibly it more relates to his being rheumaticky.

We are all blessed be God pretty well the Children are almost free of the cold, I received but five spoons for I sent but five, I think they are very pretty, I have sent a nother to change it could not be found when the rest was sent. My Lady your Mother desired me to writ to you that you would be pleased to send her a scarff, she would have it of black lutstring[46] she says she must have it three ells and a quarter you will do your best to imploy your Brother to buy it [6 words or so scratched out here] She truly stands much in need of a scarff for those she has are almost queit done, so I beg My Dearest will buy it. I must also put My Dearest in remembrance to buy a gown to Craigstons daughter Betty. I am always giving you new commissions but I know My Dearest will excuse me As for the Dipleburn I think we must leave it as it is for this year, I hope against the nixt you may prevaill with Jannet Aird to queit it, and then Hugh Baird and his Brother will take it betwixt them, for indeed ---

[undated and incomplete but the mention of spoons makes it later than 13th November 1710].

---

(46)Lutstring ; or lustring ; A fine non-lustrous taffetta (Handbook of English Costume in the eighteenth century, C.W. and P.C.Willett Cunnington). Or, Silk fabric of plain weave with lustrous finish, sometimes striped and figured but often plain, and popular for summer wear during the seventeenth to nineteenth centuries (Clothes and the Child, Anne Buck).

No.15.

My Very Dearest Sweet Heart
 I wrot to you Saturday last by Slouen which I hope
by this time you have received, I had since a letter
from My Dearest, with ane inclosed from My Aunt
Overkirk, wherin she acquaints me with the
melancholie news of poor George Cochran's death, I
have sent My Dearest her letter to read the particulars,
and you may take your own prudent way of
acquainting my Sister, and afterwards you may give her
my letter here inclosed. Poor woman I desire to
sympathise with her, Lord suport (?) her and give her
the sanctified use of all his dispensations towards
her[47]. I must truly quarrell My Dearest for not opening
the letter before you sent it me, I truly take it unkindly,
wer it not that I have so much experience to the
contrary, I would say wher ther is seremony ther is
little kindness. I shall writ to My Aunt by nixt occasion
for now I have no time. I bless God for the
comfortable account you give me of your well being,
which I assure you is the most refreshing news I can
hear. We are all blessed be God in pretty good health,
except our poor little Jamie, who since tusdays night
has been very indisposed, he took it in the midst of
the night, he seem'd not to be so sick as pain'd all that

---

(47)It is not clear who George Cochran was. Lady Mary and
    William Cochrane had no child called George, according to
    Burke, and as she must have been in her late forties by now,
    the death of an unrecorded infant, similarly to Davie Boswell,
    seems unlikely.

night and a great part of the nixt day his skin was as
cool as mine, and his pulse calm, but had great
startings, and then cry'd pitfully, and his eyes wer
extremely heavie, afterwards wensday afternoon he
turned very feverish, and all that night, and nixt day, I
sett therefore a lochlitch[48] behind his ear which
blessed be God had very good effect, for he was much
calmer afterwards, and rested well wher befor he got
almost no rest, I was jealous he was breeding the small
pox, but now the time they use to straik out being past
and the Child likways being better, I am out of that
apprehension,what his deseas is I can give it no neam,
for he has no symtom of any cold, and no appearance
of any teeth, we are jealous it may be haiv's [? hives],
for Mrs Lockhart tells me her little daughter was much
as he was and it was nothing but haiv's, I have given
him My Lady Kents pouder twice, and am to give him
the Besser Ston this evening, I never saw a Child so
shaiken with a few days sickness as he is, his eyes still
continues very heavie, but he is much easier and
smeills now and then so that I am hopeful the worst
is past: he is in the hands of a good God, who will
care for him, let us therefore My Dearest resigne him
up to Him, and how ever the Lord in his holy and
wise providence shall be pleased to dispose of him
may he give us a heart to say good is the will of God;
we and all our enjoyments are the Lords, why should
he not do with his own what he pleases.

---

(48)Lochlitch; a leech S.D. (C.)

William Templeton in Longholm was with me, he
desired I would acquaint you that he has got a
Summonds from that William Campbell of whom he
spock to you, about James Templetons intermissions,
he alledging that he was tutor[49], which William denays,
he intreats you may be pleased to let him know what
he shall do for his defence, he says he believes it is one
James Logan in the castle that advises him to it, he
thinks if you would be pleased to be at the trouble to
writ to James Logan your opinion (which William says
you told him was) that in law he could not reach him
he would diswade William not to pursue further I
intreat My Dearest may let me have your answer
hereupon by first occation. Hugh is a good tennant,
but as now the scandle is grievous [This sentence does
not seem to fit within the context, but is definitely
correctly transcribed] I hope My Dearest has written a
letter to Mr James Lourie with Samson, if you have
not I beg you may do it with the bearer, tho I am
affraid it will be ineffectual, for I find by him that
Kirkmighell is the place he will choise, however I
know not what influence your letter may have. I wish
My Dearest could prevail with My Lord Louden to
give you a right to the Patronage, I thought Mr
William Dalrymple might have been a good
instrument therefore, but I understand that he is much
picked [piqued ?] at you that you did not applay
sooner for getting Mr James Lourie to Auchinleck, for
that he apprehended you did not do it because he had

---

(49)Tutor. "A guardian appointed for a minor, whether by a
testament, or by a disposition of law" ; S.D.(J.).

recommended him to you, and this one told me that Lady Betty Crichton said the same to them, I intreat you may take your own prudent way of undeseaving him, for as he is a very good neighbour so I would desire that friendship might be keept up betwixt us, which sometimes a small thing marrs. I have sent with the bearer two shirts, one per of sleiv's, two gravats, I would have My Dearest cause flurish the gravats. I have therefore run no threeds through them for I know not when they flurish them if they run threeds through them. I hope you will be pleased to send me holland for your necks and sleiv's. I have inclosed sent a letter to Lady Betty Crichton and Lady Charles Kerr and Sir David Hamilton and My Sister you will be pleased to send them to them but as for the Lady Stenhop my Dearest must be pleased to send me a scroll if you would have me writ to her. now farewell My Sweet Dearest you will see I still fall in the same fault of troubling you with long letters for I doubt nothing of your kindly acceptance of them having so much experience of your goodness Lord be with you My Sweet Dearest and send us a comfortable meeting in his own time I am whyle I breath

My Very Dearest Heart

Auchinleck   Yours most affectionately
2nd Dec'r 17i0   Elizabeth Boswell

just now I hear that Lady Mary Crichtoun is dead Lord fitt and prepair us for the change. be pleased to give my kind service to your Brother and all friends My Dearest will be pleased to send three or four

common candlestick Mrs Hamilton has yet mony for
three of the white iron ons
I have sent My Dearest linens in a servet this is now
four servets you have one I sent with Slouen befor
you went away and two I sent with you with your
linens and now this if My Dearest has no use for them
you will please send them back

No.16.

My Sweet Dearest Heart
Since my last to you I had four of your sweet letters,
by Slouin, Samson, and two by Murdoch, all of which
wer great cordialls to me. blessed be God My Dearest
had so safe a journey, and was in so good health,
which is truly the best news I can hear, long be it so if
it is his holy will. I received all the things my Dearest
mentions and returns you many thanks, but I am sory
My Dearest should still be troubling your self to send
so many things. I return Mr Selkirk many thanks for
his cheese, I shall keep it well in hopes I may need it
for what you writ he sent it, if it wer the will of God I
should be very well satisfied, but his will be done who
knows better than we do what is fit for us. I had a
letter from Mr Mair acquainting me that my Nurse is
very ill, and in very poor circumstances, and seems to
be near death, he desired I would send her three or
four shillens, I think my Dearest may be pleased to
send Mr Mair a crown to give her, more will be
needless, if she live any time we may send her more
afterwards. Ocheltrie is not yet come here, I shall in
obedience to your desire be as kind to him as I can,
but truly other ways upon many accounts he deservs
not much kindness at our hand, one instance thereof
his determining the reference of the earrings as I see
by the paper you sent me he has done, after that I
think no honest Man should converse with him,
having it would seem cast off all faith and truth, when
My Dearest knows the horrible oaths he did swear to

you to the contrary, poor Man he is to be pittied and
my poor Sister that she is matched with such a wretch
Lord support her, and give her the sanctified use
thereof and work a change upon him for Christs sake.
what reason I have to bless God that I am not in her
case, and that he has given me not only the best of
Husbands but the best of Men, I am dayly more and
more convinced that I never deserved such a
happieness, but I am full of desire to be a good Wife.
it is very comfortable to me My Sweet Dearest that
the time is drawing so near that I hope again to enjoy
my Dearests most desireable company which much do
I long for, every day seems a month to me, Lord send
us a comfortable meeting if it be his holy will. I wrot
to My Dearest with designe to have sent my letter with
Andrew Murdoch, and sent it for that end to William
Ghrame, but Murdoch did not call at his house so the
letter was return'd to me, I send it now here inclosed,
and send also the twenty guines my Dearest left, if
you stand in need of mony to make up that soum to
Captain Broun let me know and I shall endeavour to
get you some less or more. I have also sent the linen
you left here, and the codwair that came with the
flour. be pleased to let me know My Dearest if you
have got notice of a fitt servant in Margaret Smiths
place I would have her a consciencious lass, and not
suffer[50], and that can do well with her hands, and

---

(50)"Not suffer" makes no sense here , and we possibly have
confusion with the long "s", so the word is actually "susser".
In which case S.D.(J.) gives "Sussie ; to trouble," so could this
mean someone not troublesome ?

understand to make meat rady upon occations, very
expert in peastrie, and a good dresser of muslins, I
would not have her fieed by way of a gentlewoman
but as hous keeper for the most part of those they call
gentlewomen are deir in keeping.   The shoees fitts
Sandie very well and he was very pleased with them,
the twines shoees one per of them was to big My
Dearest will be pleased to send a nother per the littlest
that can be had for Jamie has a very little foot.
Andrew Bruce desires you may send half a pund of
beans, and two pund of peas, he has been gathering
firr husks but ther are very few, he and his Brother
and John Broun has ben gathering severall days and I
believe they have not gather'd three pecks, and they
say they can get no more[51].Andrew says you will have
no more then serve you self if you sow any ---

[Incomplete and undated, but from the context of the
twins shoes, possibly November / December 1710]

---

(51)Beyond a relationship to the fir tree,"firr husks " is
   untraceable. Would fir cones have been collected for fire
   lighters ? A peck is a fourth part of a bushel, or two gallons
   (Collins Ref. Eng. Dict.).

MY VERY DEAREST SWEET HEART

No.17.

My Sweet Dearest Heart
I send here inclosed a letter I wrot to you saturday
last, and others inclosed, thinking Slouen should have
gone the monday after, but was hindered by the
badness of the weather. I received two of my Dearests
sweet letters since, by Samson and Murdoch, and all
the things you mention, and returns My Dearest many
thanks but I am truly vext you should put your self to
so much expences upon my account, I may say
without a liee my mind is not much sett upon those
things, they are raither a burthen to me, I am sure the
harness could not be cheap for they are very good, I
have according My Dearests desire sent with the
bearer a nail of every sort in the chaise, it will take half
a hunder of the biggest and a wholl hunder of the
smallest. I am sory my Dearest is so much troubled
with the gravell, Lord in his infinit mercy give you
relief, and preserve you for his glory and good of your
familie, and comfort of your poor Wife, who would
have little satisfaction upon earth if you wer gone, but
I trust the Lord will shutt my eyes before that [He did,
Elizabeth died in 1739, while James outlived her till
1749]. as for my not writing with Murdoch I had
written with Samson the day befor, and tho I could
with pleasure have written a wholle sheite againe, yet I
thought it was to much abusing your goodness to
trouble you so frequently with my scribles, when you
are so much hurried with bussiness: I am ashamed
that you should shew so much reguard to my

insignificant letters, but I cannot but own I am
extremely pleased therewith having non more
freedome to writ, in which I have great satisfaction,
for since I am deprived of the happiness of my
Dearests sweet company which is no small regrait to
me, converse by writ is nixt best, some times when I
am writing I just fancy my self speaking to my
Dearest, which is no small satisfaction as you may
judge; I do not think my Dearest in earnest that I
should be so much taken up with our Children and
familie as to forget the comfort of my life, so shall
give no reply therto. As for my going to Edinburgh I
hope I have satisfied My Dearest in the inclosed ther
anent, but I must redouble my earnest requeist that
you may not come here befor the session raise, I have
a perfect terrour in my mind about it, considering the
badness of the season, and to stay so short a time
befor you be rested to be gone. So I hope My Dearest
to ease my mind will promise me that you will not
come. I have written to My Lady Overkirk and Lady
Stenhop and have sent you them here inclosed, I
return you many thanks for the scroll which pleases
me extremely. I sent Mr Lourie his letter I suppose he
has written a reply therto, I hear it has great weight
with him, and that he resolve's to refer it wholly to the
Presbitery to determine the matter, some is afraid the
presbytery will favour Kirkmighell, I have written to
Mr Henry Osburn, and Mr Cummine, and Mr
Kennedie, the last Presbitery, Mr Osburn and Mr
Cummine appear'd very much our friend. Uncle is
still with us, he is the most harmless pleasant company

that can be, he is speaking nothing of going away, so I am hopefull he may stay yet some time. My Dearest must be pleased to writ to him and return him thanks for his having stay'd so long. My Lady your Mother was speaking againe to me about her scarff so I intreat My Dearest may buy it. if I needed any thing to myself you may assure your self I would writ freely to you for it so I intreat you may send me nothing but when I writ for it. Andrew Bruce desires you may send a trap for taking meiss for they are like to fall upon the beis sceaps[52], he is making use in the mein time of my litle trap, which has already taken three. My Dearest will be pleased also to send a mup for muping up the rooms. I am truly sory for My Lady Dondonall Lord fitt and prepair us we see young diec as well as old death passes non by when it gets its commission. we have indeed no small reason as My Dearest very well says to bless God who has preserved our little sweet infants in that dangerous desease which cuts off so many, Lord help us to true thankfullness for all his innumerable mercys blessed be God we are all here in pretty good health, the Children are now perfectly free of the cold, little Sandie grows every day a finer Child, he speaks often of his dear Papa. I have nothing of that which you apprehend. I would be glad to know if Hanna Seaton be to stay still in her service, for if she be not I think we may take her or if My Dearest incline raither for a nother I am satisfied for I find I must part with

---

(52)Mice attacking the bee hives

Margret besides she does not incline to stay but I must
say she has been a faithfull and honest servant, I wish
we may get one that may be as faithfull every one is
not for us therefore My Dearest has great need to
chois well.   Andrew Bruce is very diligent I hope My
Dearest will be well satisfied when you come home
with his work I recomend to him frequently to look to
the dycks, I think he is very carefull now farewell My
Dearest the Lord be with you I am

My Sweet Dearest Heart

Auchinleck   yours most affectionately
9 Dec'r 1710   Elizabeth Boswell

Andrew Slouen was speaking to me to writ to you that
you would be so good to contrebute some thing
among your acquaintances you know he had a loss of
mony stollen from him you may speak to my Sister for
him also

No.18.

My Dearest Sweet Heart
I have yours by Mr Blair, as also one since by Slouen,
and all the things My Dearest mentions to have sent,
blessed be God for the good news of the continuance
of your well being, which is refreshing to me beyond
expression. I return My Dearest many thanks for your
mindfullness about my commissions, all is very right,
and very good, but Veties shoees are to big, both to
long and over widd by a great deal, so I have sent
them back. I have not sent back the cusk seeing you
writ you will return it againe full and I think My
dearest has sent anough I hope to make it serve a
great wheill, they say ther is very good kenaire [canary
(wine)?] at Glasgow[53], when we get occation we may
send the cusk ther for some, but ther is no heast.
Ocheltrie was here last Saturday at dinner, and stayed
all night, and all Sabath for he durst not go to the
Church being troubled with a loussness, but he went
away in the evening for he was afraid he would not
have got through the water nixt day it being a great
thaw,[54] and he had Coudom and all his tennants
trysted, so that ther was a necessity for his going, I
have not seen him since, but I will see to get him to
stay for a night or two with us before he leave the

---

(53) "Glasgow = Place of the green hollow. --- Glasgow remained a small,
pretty cathedral city until well into the eighteenth century" ; David Ross,
"Scottish Place-names"
(54) The way to the "Old Place" seems to have crossed the Lugar
by a ford before Lord Auchinleck's Barony Road – the "Via
Sacra".

Countrie, I hear he continues his old tread in John
Donalds, poor Man he is to be pittied, I long to hear
how My Sister is and what is doing in their bussiness
with Ca: [Captain?] Areskine. pray let me know if the
Presidents marriage be going with Lady Bangour.   I
have sent here a list of what seeds Andrew Bruce
desires. I have here sent our Sandies measure as you
desired, My Dearest will be pleased to cause make
what is most fashionable, I believe indeed a poloman
will be fittest for him[55], he stands much in need of it,
for he is perfectly disfigur'd with the clouths he has,
and it is a pitie for I must say he is a fine little Man.
the little twines grows every day pleasanter Children,
James cheek is now perfectly well he is as like you as a
Child can be and you may believe I like him not the
worse. I am heartily glad My Sweet Dearest has been
detained from comeing here, it is to long a journey to
make once in a winter for so short a stay, and much
more then to make twice. the time is now drawing fast
on that I hope to enjoy My Sweet Dearest company
for a longer time, which indeed much do I long for.
now My Dearest I must be much shorter than I
intended having been hinder'd from writing all day by
company and now it is late, and I am wearie not being
very well, but I hope befor this come to My Dearests
hand I will be better so I intreat you may take no
thoughts about me. All the rest in this familie blessed
be God are in their ordinary, little Vetie was ill of the

---

(55) S.D.(J.) gives "Polonie, Polonaise : A dress for very young
   boys [Sandie was at this time four and a half], including a
   sort of waistcoat with loose sloping skirts"

cold but blessed be God she is better, she and little
Sandie gives their dear Papa their humble duty. I
forgot to take Sandies measure and now he is in bed,
but I shall send it with nixt occation which I believe
will be very shortly, for I hear Andrew Murdoch goes
upon tusday.   I intreat My Dearest may not send
above one loaf, I have now wheat of our own which I
am going to grind, and I hope it will make very good
bread, and I hope we may make our own product
serve us   ther is one of your mears not well it is
?Loghtong she first took the ?balls, but now she has a
very ill cold, I am affraid she turn like your last brown
gelden for she has a geathering at her choiks[56], and
cast a great deall out at her nose. I am thinking if she
grow no better to send her to Glasgow to Swan, we
shall neglect no means, George Murdoch is affraid you
think he has neglected her, but he says he could do no
more if it were for his life she has only casted this two
days the thing that she casts out is white. She has queit
lost her stomach, she eats nothing almost, George
thinks that her choicks is bealing[57] and that is the
reason she can not eat.   Mr Henry Osburn is here he
is to preach for us tomorrow he gives you his humble
and kind service, please give mine to all friends.

---

(56) S.D.(J.) gives "Chokkeis pronounced *chouks* , the jaws;
properly the glandular parts under the jaw-bones".
(57)S.D.(J.) : "suppurating" ; it seems the poor horse had a
salivary gland infection.

farewell My Dearest Heart, the Lord be with you, and
send us a comfortable meeting if it be his holy will I
am whyle I live

                        My Sweet Dearest Heart
Auchinleck   Yours most affectionately
16 Dec'r   Elizabeth Boswell
   1710

I have written to my Sister that I have sent you my
letter from My Lady Overkirk to communicat to her
the contents thereof I know not if it will be proper to
give her the letter because of what she writs about
Ocheltrie.
17 Dec'r My Dearest I thought fitt to acquaint you
that blessed be God our little Jamie has rested this
night and continues to be better

CHAPTER 4 :
EDINBURGH AND THE LAW

As almost all the letters are addressed to James in Edinburgh, a few notes on that city in the early eighteenth century will not be out of place. T.C.Smout in "A History of the Scottish People, 1560 - 1830", (p.276), gives some very useful information : -

"Lawyers were the intellectual linchpin of Edinburgh society after 1707" and (p.146) "Edinburgh at the end of the seventeenth century held upwards of 30,000 inhabitants and therefore vied with Bristol, the second city of England: even so it was no more populous than modern Dumfries or Airdrie, and so compact in its tall crowded tenements and narrow wynds as to cover an area no more than one mile long and a quarter of a mile wide [i.e., the environs of what is now known as the Royal Mile from the Castle to Holyrood Palace] --- (p.151) In sanitary matters the feebleness of municipal government was still more serious. It was normal for the population to dispose of their sewage by throwing it out of the window to the cry of 'gardy loo'. A more sophisticated method was to build a closet jutting over one of the wynds, so that the excrement would fall directly on to the heads of pedestrians and not foul the walls. At best the sewage was piled in heaps at the edge of the road".

This then was the more than somewhat unsavoury environment in which James senior would have found himself. And things had obviously not improved by 1773, when James his grandson wrote in "The Journal of a Tour to the Hebrides with Samuel Johnson Ll.D." (p.11) : -

"Doctor Johnson and I walked arm in arm up the High Street to my house in James Court: it was a dusky night: I could not prevent his being assailed by the effluvia of Edinburgh", - and Johnson made the comment - "I smell you in the dark, Boswell".

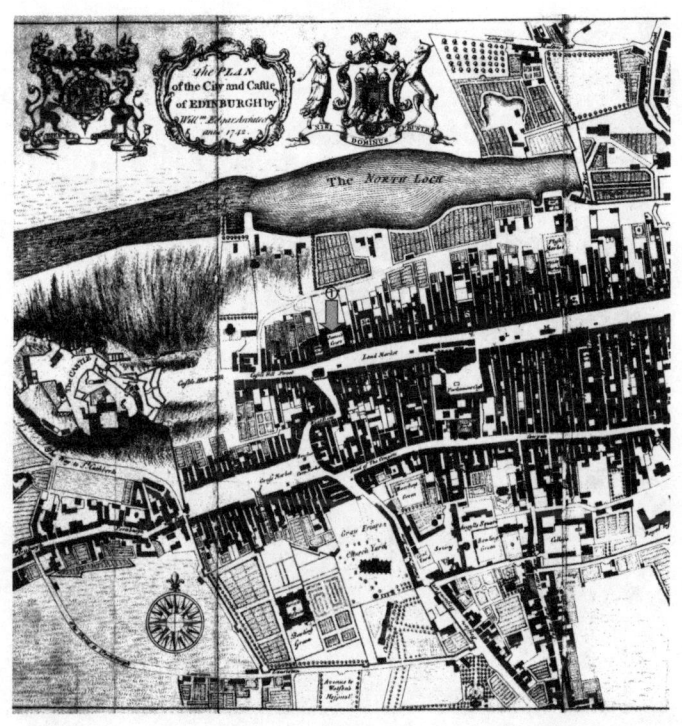

PLATE 17 : MAP OF WEST EDINBURGH (1742) BY
WILLIAM EDGAR, WITH (1) JAMES' COURT

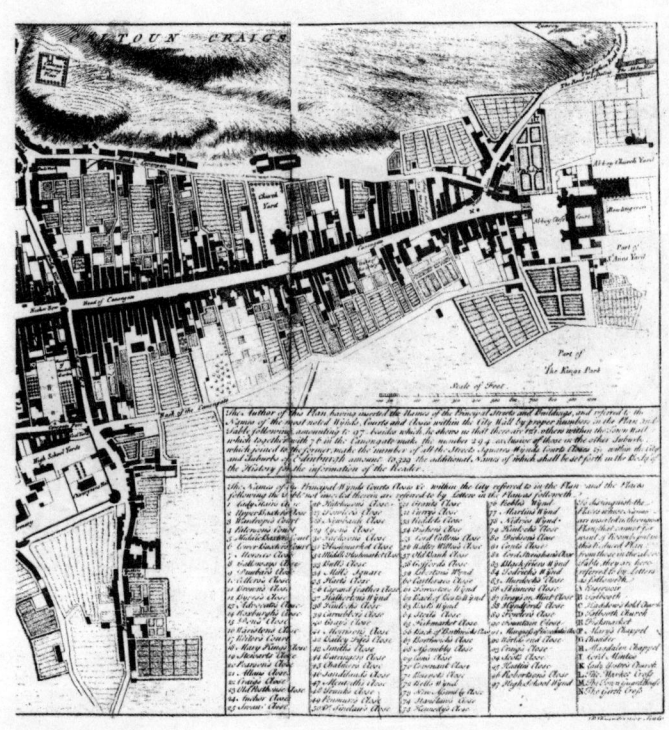

PLATE 18 : MAP OF EAST EDINBURGH (1742) BY
WILLIAM EDGAR

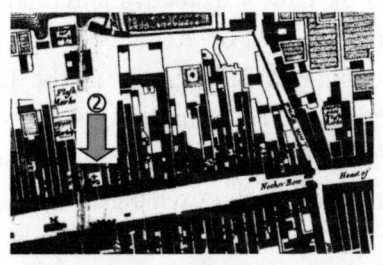

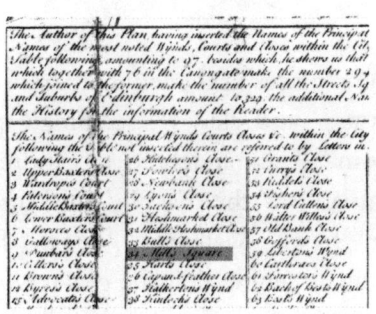

PLATE 19 : ENLARGEMENT OF CENTRAL
EDINBURGH AND STREET KEY SHOWING (2) MILLS
SQUARE

J.A.C.Boswell's family history has told that James senior had "written" in Crawford of Crawfordjohn's Chambers till 1695, prior to his studying Civil Law at Leyden. Two of Lady Elizabeth's letters are addressed "To Mr. James Boswell of Auchinleck Advocat at Mrs Craufurds lodging in Mills Squer in the Landmarkett [Lawnmarket] att Edinburgh", No.34 on the Edinburgh map. Could this be the wife or widow of the same Crawford ? The exchange of gifts suggests a possibly more than merely landlady - tenant relationship. And we know James senior eventually bought a house in the city. Could it have been Mrs Crawford's ?

In several places in the letters there is mention of "necks, gravats, and sleiv's", seemingly part of the legal "uniform". I am indebted to Andrea Longson, Senior Librarian of the Faculty of Advocates, for information from Walker's "Legal History of Scotland", vol. V, stating that the gown worn in Court had "bell sleeves fastened up to the elbow and bands worn hanging from the collar to a little above the waist". This accounts for the sleiv's, and probably the necks. Was the cravat more elaborate and "frothy" such as is worn by the Lord Chancellor today, and possibly part of what might be called, in Services jargon, the No.1 Uniform for legal formal or official occasions?

Collins Encyclopaedia of Scotland (Ed. John Keay and Julia Keay) gives some useful information on the position of the Scottish legal system at the period when James Boswell was in legal practice as an advocate, just after the turn of the eighteenth century:-

> p.602 "Although the kingdoms had shared a monarch since 1603 their political, legal and social systems remained distinct if converging. Attempts to negotiate a union met with no success until the passing of the **Alien Act** 1705 concentrated the minds of Scots Parliamentarians. The Parliaments appointed Commissioners and in 1706 negotiations took place in London leading to agreement on --- the judicial system --- The treaty of **Union** made specific provision for the preservation of the Scottish Legal System. Article XIX provides 'that the Court of Session or College of Justice do after the Union and notwithstanding thereof remain in all time coming within Scotland, and that the Court of Justiciary do also after the Union also after the Union --- remain in all time coming' "

And, p.603 : -

> "Law and the Universities

> The development of Scots Law in the post-Union period was the outstanding achievement of Scottish jurists and judges.

It coincided in great measure with that flowering of arts, literature and philosophy which constituted the **Scottish Enlightenment** - an epoch of intellectual activity on a grand scale embracing almost every field of human endeavour and contributing in no small way to the concept of modern civilization. This climate allowed the emergence of Scots law as a university taught discipline --- effective law teaching was not commenced in the Scottish universities after the Reformation and students continued to go abroad, particularly to Leyden or Utrecht in Holland ---"

It will be remembered, James himself went to Leyden, as did his sons, Alexander for his law studies similarly, and John for his medical postgraduate studies, and his grandson James the biographer was to go to Utrecht for law study, prior to his 'Grand Tour' of Europe and the beginnings of his literary career. However, it seems Holland was also regarded as a place of exile, or shelter from uncomfortable circumstances – Alexander Bruce had been in Holland with the future Charles II. And Dane Love tells us, p.46, that John Cochrane of Waterside, younger brother of "Ocheltrie", "took part in the Battle of Bothwell Bridge on 22nd June 1679, fighting for the Covenanters, even though he was just sixteen years old. He subsequently fled to Holland with his father, but returned in 1685 when he was active in the

Monmouth and Argyle insurrection".

"--- In Edinburgh law teaching had originally been undertaken by way of private tuition by advocates ---The university began teaching law only in the first decade of the eighteenth century".

Letters No. 19 to 22 (1710 & 1711)
No. 19.

My Very Dearest Sweet Heart
I had yours by Mr Osburns servant, I bless God for
the comfortable acount of the continuance of your
well being, long be it so if it be his holy will. I hope
My Dearest will not hold your resolution of coming
here befor the session raise I am so much afraid of
your being the worse by your heastie journeys here,
and back, that I rather choise to go to you if other
ways you will not be deverted, I cannot tell you how
uneasie I am about your coming, therefore I most
earnestly intreat againe you may not come. I am glad
to hear Lady Charles Kerr is safely brought to bed,
she is a young Mother of six Children. I shall be glad
it be a ?fallie [?false] report that George Cochrane is
kiled, I thought ther was no doubt of it by what My
Lady Overkirk wrott, ellse I would not have been so
rady to have written to my poor Sister, for indeed I
love not to be a first teller of ill news, especially to
those I love and respect, but I thought I was obliged
to do it seeing my Aunt had written it to me. I am
afraid it but be to true, for I think if it had been other
ways he would have written himself befor now. I wish
My Dearest would be pleased to send me back my
Aunts letter, for I cannot well answer it befor I have it.
I sent both to Gleenlie and William Ghrame for firr
feed, William Ghrame has non, Gleenlies Gardiner
will not part with any he has tho I made offer him

113

considerably more for it back againe when the time
comes for gathering it, Gleenlie is very unwell himself
so that he could not be spock to about it. I am afraid
he is dieing, the Doctor is droging on with him, and
his Sister Mrs Luke is come to wait on him, he grows
the longer the worse, he seems to be in a decay. I am
truly concerned for him, we will loss a very discreit
kind neighbour, I hear he is very serious, and much
concerned for his soul. Lord help us whyle prepairing
for death, for when sickness comes it often times
incapacitats us therefore. I had a letter from Mr Mair,
he seems to be very concerned for our happie
settlement of our vacancie in this place, and for that
end recommends one Mr Robert Willocks who at
present is at Ed'r as he writs, I believe he is the same
Mr Logan spock to you about, My Dearest may
enqueir about him, I doubt not but Mr Webster may
know him, but indeed ther is non I incline to so much
as Mr Logan, but I am affraid it will be labour in vain
to seek after him, Lord send us one according to his
own heart.   Since writing this I had My Dearests by
Samson and returns My Dst many thanks for not
neglecting writ tho so much hurried with bussiness, it
is more then I deserve that you should be so mindfull
of me, I bless God for the good news of My Dearests
well being. I bless God we are all in our ordinary little
Jamie has been much better this three days but he has
as yet got out no teeth, but Johne has got out one
perfectly, and another almost out, I have a per of
shoees for Jamie My Dearest will be pleased to send a
per to Johne; they must be for a Child of half a year

old, he has not a large foot, he is a very sprightly little
Man, we knew not that he was breeding teeth till we
saw the teeth, for he was no ways sick as for the night
goun I would have sent it back but I am afraid the
weather be not yet very settel'd so that it may be
spoiled, but My Dearest wherefore do you say you will
bay a nother I am sure that I stand in need of non
having more then I think I will ever wear, therefore I
most earnestly beseech you do not vex me in either
doing or writting such thing. I assure you My Dearest
what I writ to you in all sincerity and no complement,
I say not the half of what I think upon that heed. I
am heartily sory to hear Ocheltrie continues his sad
manner of life, Lord work a change upon him, my
Sister is much to be pittied Lord suport her. My
Dearest writs me no answer about William Templeton
in Longholms bussiness nor if I shall sett the half of
the ?Woodmock to George Templeton, it is no
wonder if My Dst forget when you have such a
multitude of bussiness, but if My Dearest can
conveniently I wish you may let me know by your nixt.
My Lady your Mother is not pleased that her scarff is
not come, I told her your Brother was all to blame, for
that you had writ to me that you had desired him to
bay it, I intreat it may not be neglected to be sent at
this time with the bearer she desires it may be of
lutstring, three ells and a quarter. The geiss are not so
good as I would have them so have delay'd sending

them till nixt occasion now farewell My Sweet Dearest
the Lord be with you, and in his own time send us a
comfortable meeting, I ever am

My Very Dearest Sweet Heart

Auchinleck   Yours most affectionately

6 Jan'ry   Elizabeth Boswell

1711

Be pleased to give my very kind service to your
Brother and to all friends. your Father and Mother
remembers you very kindlie and Sandie and Vetie
gives their humble dutie to their dear Papa

No. 20.

My Very Dearest Sweet Heart
I long for ane account of your safe journey to
Edinburgh, and that you are not the worse thereof,
which will be most refreshing news to me. it mar's
much the satisfaction I would have of having seen My
Dearest the fear I have that you may be the worse, I
was much rejoyced you got so good weather, I hope
you reatched your journeys [end] the time you
designed. pray let me have a particular account how
you are, and if you have had any loss in your bussiness
by being absent. I bless God we continue in our
ordinary, only little Johne has not been so very well
this two three days, I think he is breeding more teeth.
I have sent with the bearer Samson four geiss, ther are
two of them very good, they are in the servet marked
E.B. i7i0, I think you will give them to Mr Selkirk, the
other two are also pretty good, but ther is one better
then the other. I was seeing Glenliee upon wensday,
he is truly very ill, I am apprehensive he will not
overcome it, he is altogether spent, he looks like a
goost ! yet he told me he is free of a cough, and has
no drouth, but has no manner of appeteit, all he can
take is a little bear meal pottage[58], I advised him to get
ane ass, for that I thought the milk would be very
proper for him, he seem'd much inclined therto
himself, and said he would perhaps send for one, but I
hear since Doctor Cobron who is the phesitian he

---

(58)Drouth; thirst. Bear; barley, having four rows of grains.
    Pottage; --- broth with vegetables in it . All from S.D.(J.).

makes use of advises him raither to make use of womens milk. I sent him yesterday a receipt for geel of harts horn which he desired, he sent me word he was no better but raither worse. he asked kindly for you. My Dearest will be pleased to let me know what shall be done with the Ministers Gleib, if it shall be left, I think Mrs Lourie may be allowed to stay in the house, till we get a Minister, for she will keep it right, besyds it will be a kindness done to her which she deserv's very well, both upon her own account and her worthie husbands. I hope My Dearest has sent My Lady your Mothers scarff with Slouen, if you have not I intreat you may send it with the bearer, and Sandies shoees if they be rady, and a per of shoees to Vetie I have sent one of her shoees for a pattern, but they must be a little larger every way, but especially longer they may be near ane einch longer. I beg My Dearest may be pleased to cause enqueir at the wever how much of my yearon he saw for damask must be for warp and how much for waft I mean how many cuts for the elle. I beg My Sweet Dearest a thousand pardons for troubling you with so many triffels I abuse of your goodness. I shall trouble My D'st no further at this time, but pray God be with you, and in his time send us a comfortable meeting, which I long much for. I am as much as I am capable

My Sweet Dearest
Yours most affectionately whyle
Elizabeth Boswell

Auchinleck
15 Jan'ry
1711

be pleased to give my kind service to your Brother and all friends as if named I desire my damask to be at least three quarters and a half broad and I would have it very thick wrought so that the weaver must consider that when he tells how much yearon he must have for the ells warp and waft

No. 21.

My Very Dearest Sweet Heart
I wrot this day by James Samson I am glad of this
occation of Murdoch againe to salute my Sweet
Dearest, I think I could with pleasure writ every day to
My D'st if occation serv'd. I was hopefull to have
heard from My D'st from Slouen befor this, the
weather has been so good I doubted not but he would
have been here saturday or at least early this day, but
he is not as yet come, I never longed more for him
being anxious to hear how you got in, Lord send me
good news if it be his holy will.Mitchell in Braehead
was with me, he presses mightily that you would sett
that piece of land ?in the Hemp [slightly unclear as
written between lines] that you sett this year in grass,
he brought a young Man with him that is satisfied to
take it, one Crichtoun who I suppose Married a Neece
of his, Hugh Murdoch went alongs with him to look
to the ground, he seems to be very forward to take it,
and I believe would be satisfied to give three bolls for
it[59], Braehead promices much for Crichtons
responsableness but Hugh Murdoch has no great
opinion of him, for he says he is a young Man and has
gon through fast what he had, I would do nothing
therin till I should have My Dearests orders, Mitchell
says the Haugh people destroys all his corn, and that if
you will not sett it to Crichtoun he wishes you would

---

(59) Westminster Eng. Dict. gives boll as "an old measure of two
    to six bushels or 140 lbs avoirdupois". But in this context it
    must surely be a financial transaction.

sett it to another, I intreat My Dearest may let me have your answer by the first occation. I have not time to writ now to Lady Charles Kerr but I shall writ by first occation, pray let me know how she and her familie are, and how my poor Sister is, I hope you have now got up that paper from Charles he promised you, if you have not I think My D'st should seek it. I have not time now to add more it being late, all here send their very kind service to you, particularly Uncle, who intreats you may be pleased to give him a return to his letter he sent with Samson tho it should be never so short. Vetie and Sandie gives their humble duty to their dear Papa I am

My Very Dearest Sweet Heart

Auchinleck	Yours most affectionately
15 Jan'ry	Elizabeth Boswell
1711	

[on back cover]: -

To

Jan 15	
1711	Mr James Boswell of
	Auchinleck Advocat
	Att Edinburgh

No. 22.

[This is a bit of a puzzle. It is clearly the last sheet of a letter. The respective sheets of previous letters follow a definite pattern; written in two columns on a folded sheet, right hand page, no.1, over the page to left side, no.2, to right, no.3, and back over again to left side, with no.4 adjacent to no.1. In this case, following this pattern, the footnote "ther is no feed -" is not followed on by the other side "blessed be God"---].

--- Ocheltrie is now come he came straight here and stay'd about two hours I was as kind to him as I could be he has promised to come nixt week and stay a night or two, I am sory to hear by him that my Sister is very ill of rumatick pains he says she fell ill that same night she came to Culross and has keept her bed ever since her poor Children would have a great loss if any thing shoud ail her which God forbid, now farewell My Dearest I am loath to give over writing but that I have yet severall letters to writ and it is already late I have been deverted all day from writing with company I am

My Dearest Sweet

Auchinleck   Yours with inexpressible
27 Jan'ry   affection
1711   Elizabeth Boswell

Ther is no feed here that I can hear of that is any thing worth I wish My Dearest would ---

MY VERY DEAREST SWEET HEART

[over the page] : -

--- blessed be God we are all in pretty good health
little Jamie was a little uneasie this week with a boill at
his cheek near his ear which brock this night so I hope
it will soon be well, and that he will be much the
better

My Dearest will be pleased to send some thing to be a
collour'd frock to both the twines I would have it
some strong thing that will wash well I think blew
stamped calligo will be best for the ?ried/reed does
not keep[60], it needs not be fine for it is for ordinary
wearing, the white frocks lasts not a moment clean I
believe such frock will take two ells for I desire as
much as be two bodies to each for they wear soon I
send here inclosed a match of your Fathers coat I am
to cause make for him My Dearest will be pleased to
send buttons and hair for it.

---

(60) Possibly, red is not colour fast. Also, could "blew calligo" be
the original denim ?

Chapter 5: Estate Business

The letters contain much discussion of agricultural and estate matters and concerning estate staff. Andrew Bruce seems to have been the estate factor/head gardener. David Buchanan in the "Treasures of Auchinleck" mentions some letters, lost in the U.S.A., which included letters from James Bruce, "overseer at Auchinleck" [with whose daughter Euphemia, chamber maid in the house and named after James' mother, James junior had had a flirtation (Boswell, The Earlier Years, 1740-1769, F.A.Pottle, p. 289)]. And Pottle also mentions James Bruce's father as having been a "trusted servant of the house". Going back a further generation to that of James senior and Andrew Bruce, it seems this was a dynasty of Bruce gardeners and overseers or factors on the estate. However it ended during the lifetime of the biographer, with James Bruce being succeeded by Andrew Gibb. In Auchinleck Kirk graveyard, close to the Boswell Mausoleum, there is a gravestone to "Andrew Bruce, gardner to Auchinleck" who died 1742 (? as the stone is rather weathered). This date would seem appropriate for people of James senior's generation.

In Letter No.16, probably November/December 1710, Lady Elizabeth sends James a list of Andrew Bruce's seed requirements for the vegetable garden. But in No.27, 27th February 1711, it sounds as if poor

James has been conned over the seeds. Perhaps, being apparently more of a "city type" he had little gardening knowledge.

There is mention of "Firr husks" being harvested, and apparently in short supply, with Elizabeth being unable to borrow some from the neighbour's gardener. There is no clue to the use of these, whether they were some type of animal fodder, or could they be fir cones used as fire-lighters?

The suggested dietary treatment for the above mentioned neighbour Glenlie is of interest ["I am very apprehensive he will not overcome it, he is altogether spent, he looks like a goost! --- all he can take is a little bear meal pottage"] – and Elizabeth suggests asses' milk, "for that I thought the milk would be very proper for him, he seem'd much inclined therto himself", but her advice is overridden "but I hear since Doctor Cobron (?Cockburn) who is the phesitian he makes use of advises him raither to make use of womens milk". The outcome of Glenlies' illness is among much unfinished history in the letters.

In No. 13, 25th November 1710 it appears the vegetable garden is being redesigned " Andrew desires to know if you will have your Nurserie at the side of the avenew where you designed --- as for levelling of the green all is of oppinion that the pend [S.D.(C.) gives various kinds of stonework, and S.D.(J.),an arch] should first be made, because it will take a vast deall of earth to lay upon it, so what will be taken off to leavell the green may be used for that effect --- let me know if I shall cause make the pend or not". So some kind of stone structure, apparently covered with earth, but for what, and was it ever built?

Transport of mail and goods is an interesting topic to consider. In almost all the letters there is recurrent mention of at least one of four names – James Samson, Andrew Slouen, James Murray, and Andrew Murdoch – in connection with sending or receipt of letters between Elizabeth and James, and in many of goods of various kinds. So the question arises of whether these were postal employees or local carriers [I am much indebted to Bath Postal Museum for the following information] : -

1) " In 1695 the Scottish parliament established a General Post Office in Edinburgh and fixed a rate of postage of three shillings for a single letter travelling over fifty miles (four shillings if over a hundred miles).

2) A so-called 'Bishop-mark' was stamped on letters received or passing through Edinburgh. This was oval in shape, with an abbreviation for the month plus day of receipt e.g., MY4 for 4th May. However Bishop-marks on letters dated between 1693 and about 1720 are very scarce.

3) If sent through the post, the letters written by your 8x grandmother would not have been in envelopes. The probability is that they would have been folded, with address on the outside and sealed with wax. It is possible that there would be a handwritten 3/- (difficult to read/decipher) and improbably a Bishop-mark

4) If sent privately e.g. via a carrier, the letter would certainly not have postal markings and it might or might not have an indication of being carried within an outer 'wrapper'.

This information makes it quite obvious that the letters were transported by local carriers as there is no sign of a "Bishop-mark" on any of the letters. In any case, three shillings sounds an immense price, something approaching twenty pounds at present values, and one would imagine not many people could afford this for routine correspondence, and especially not one of Elizabeth's degree of frugality as it appears in the letters.

In England the postal service was very haphazard until the 1720's when Ralph Allen was appointed in charge and greatly improved the system, not least by the introduction of cross-posts. Prior to this all mail had to travel into London by one of six main radial routes and back out again similarly.

In one of the letters a William Ghrame [?Graham] is named; was he a possible employer of the four carriers?

There is also an interesting social nuance to be picked up. In most mentions of their names they are merely called by the surname, Samson, etc. But where a personal friend is taking a letter we have, e.g., "The enclosed was wrot to have been sent with George Cochrane, but he was gone" [probably 19th July 1708], and also "I have yours by Mr Blair, as also one since by Slouen---" [16th December 1710].

Then in No. 12, undated but possibly autumn 1708, not only is Jannet Aird being rather cantankerous about her tenancy of the Dipleburn, but we seem to have a whiff of scandal in her relationship with Hugh Baird, of which Elizabeth with her strong religious views would clearly disapprove. The Dipleburn is possibly a mill - "the mealen in good condition so that she is able to pay her rent", so obviously a source of income [vide French moulin = mill? But certainly we have "To meal = To produce meal; applied to grain" (S.D.(J.). However the only mill marked on the map is Affleck Mill, on the River Lugar, and over a mile south of the Dippol Burn]. There is then in No. 14, again undated but probably late 1710, "As for the Dipleburn I think we must leave it as it is for this year, I hope against the nixt you may prevaill with Jannet Aird to queit it, and then Hugh Baird and his Brother will take it betwixt them, for indeed ---". Another incomplete and unsolved mystery. Though at any rate, the relationship between Hugh Baird and the obstinate Jannet seems to have fizzled out, if one can interpret this in such a way.

While discussing these matters, Smout has a very useful section on seventeenth to eighteenth century agriculture, some of which is relevant and interesting :-

> p.118 "Infield was [land] fertile enough to bear grain crops year after year without ever enjoying a fallow break --- [and] was the division that carried the drink crop of the community, bear, or four-rowed barley, that was sown in spring (in April in the south of Scotland) some three weeks after the ground had been ploughed. This normally occupied a third or a quarter of the total infield land --- giving an average return ---of something like four or five grains to every one sown. After harvesting --- the bear was generally malted and consumed in the household --- Bear, though eaten as meal in an emergency, was reckoned a very inferior food except as a potgrain to put in the broth" - and this of course was the manner in which Elizabeth recommended it for her sick neighbour Glenlie.

Again in Letter No. 21 Elizabeth writes" Mitchell --- presses mightily that you would sett that piece of land ? in the Hemp that you sett this year in grass", and Smout states: -

"Flax and hemp too was an infield crop --- every family spinning its own ropes and making its own linen according to necessity" - [In Dorset large areas of hemp were grown for nautical use, for making sails and rope].

Auchinleck flax was used for some table linen we have, made in 1710, so in Lady Elizabeth's time, with the date woven into the fabric, and still in remarkably good condition.

Letters No. 23 to 28 (1711)

No. 23.

--- I intreat you may not neglect to inqueir about a woman in Margret Smiths place for ther is a necessity for me to part with Margret as I told you when you was here besyds she is not strong and we stand in need of a strong healthy woman in that station but above all we stand in need of one that has the principall of the fear of God which only makes a faithfull servant. I intreat you againe My Dearest send but one loaf, and send non with Murdoch they coust you deir in baying, and they coust almost the half of their worth for carrage, one will abundantly serve for extrodinary strangers, and for others the flour we have will serve very well, and for sugar and rasins and those sort of things I get them as cheap and good at Kilmarnock and they coust nothing for carrage. My Dearest needs make no appologie for sending for the gold you obliged me mightilie therby very well farewell My Dearest the Lord be with you and send us a comfortable meeting if it be his holy will I am

	My Very Dearest Sweet Heart
Auchinleck	Yours most affectionately
10 Feb'ry	beyond expression
1711	Elizabeth Boswell

Be pleased to give my kind service to all friends. Be pleased to send me one unce of fige blew for blewing linens.

Your Father remembers himself most affectionatly to
you be pleased My Dearest to send me a little hinging
lock such as they put upon clog bags

[written along two edges of the sheet] : -

Souens [soon ?] blessed be God who provids so
liberally to us I am to send your Sister Treesbanks
@rent to her the nixt week for your Sister Treesbank
wrot to me that she did not desire it, and I assure you
I take a great deal of pleasure in paying principall

No. 24.

My Sweet Dearest Heart
I wrot you Saturday last with James Samson, I take
occation againe to salut My Dearest with Andrew
Murdoch, for it would be a pleasure to me to writ
every day, had I occation, and the more that I think it
would not be unaiceptable to my Sweet Dearest. I
hope to hear by the bearer the comfortable account of
your well being, which is the most refreshing news
that I can hear, as for me I cannot say I am yet very
well, but I hope I will grow better, I have as yet used
nothing, for I heat [?hate] drougs but if I grow no
better I will take some thing, I am in some case like
the Lady Watersyde was, for this three weeks I have
been that way, but not in extream, yet never free, I
past four or five days my ordinary time befor, I intreat
My Dearest take no thought about me I hope ther will
be no hazerd.
I have now sent Sandies measure, Uncle took it so I
believe it will be very exact, I think drouget[61] will be
the best thing you can make the coat of, it is a great
follie to make it of any deir thing, for both he cannot
keep it, and then if it please God to spair him he will
soon wear from it, he is not a little pleased that he is
to get a coat and buttons, he is a sturdie pleasant child,
Lord spair him if it be his holy will and make him his
servant, and a comfort to his dear Papa. I have here

---

(61) Drouget; as "Drugget , a coarse woollen cloth" (Handbook
of English Costume in the Eighteenth Century, C.W. and P.C.
Cunning ton).

inclosed sent My Dearest a letter, I believe it be from
our Session about a Minister, Lord derect to the
choise of a good on, for we stand much in need, I
would be glad to know if you have made any tryall
about Mr Allen Logan, I cannot let my mind go upon
a nother, but indeed I think it is a mercy we do not
deserve I intreat My Dearest you may use your
endeavour about it, and if that will not do you may
take Mr Websters advice about some young Man. Mr
Hugh Logan and others about the head of the Parish
I hear are much taken up with Mr Lang in
Craufurdjohn, but ther is non that will appear in it till
they know your mind, I shall say no more but pray
that the Lord may derect to one according to his own
heart, the choise of a Minister is not a light matter for
often like Prist like people.
when my yearon is rady I think I will send it to
Margret Kerr who I know will be carefull about it so
My Dearest will be pleased to speak to her about it
but I must know exactly how much warp the elle will
take you know the Weaver has already seen the yearon
it is about two speinell [? spindle] in the pund. now
farewell My Dearest the Lord be with you and send us
a comfortable meeting if it be his holy will which
much do I long for I am

My Sweet Dearest Heart

Auchinleck   Yours most affectionatly beyond
12 Feb,ry 1711   what I can express
Elizabeth Boswell

be pleased to give my kind service to your Brother and

all friends. The Children I bless God are very well I
wish My Dearest would cause seek for a mastive for
help is become so scabed that we will be obliged to
sheut him for fear he do hurt to the horses or cows

No. 25.

My Very Dearest Heart

I have not time to say much having but just now heard
of the bearer William Smith being to go, and he is
heasting to be gone, he being to take his journey this
night. I was glad of the occation for to give you ane
account that blessed be God we are all save one in
pretty good health, I am now free of that trouble
wherof I wrot to you in my last, but it has pleased
God to lay his hand upon our little sweet Johne, he
has been extreamly ill since friday last, a great fever of
cold, we have taken blood of him with a Lochlitch
and given him severall remedies but I cannot say he is
any thing better, only I think his defluction[62] is not so
great, but he is heart sick to be free with you My
Dearest I am very apprehensive of him, he is in the
hand of a tender harted Physitian, and My Dearest let
us resigne him up to him who gave him to us, I bless
his holy name he has in some measure helped me to
do so. now I have time to add no more, I hope My
Dearest will minde your poor Wife and little infants at
the throne of grace farewell

---

(62) Westminster Eng. Dict. gives "a flowing down of humours,"
and for humour, "formerly fancied to depend on the
condition of the fluids of the body."

My Dearest the Lord be with you and if it be his holy
will prevent fears and send us a comfortable meeting I
am

My Very Dearest Heart

Auchinleck   Yours most affectionatly whyle
i9 Feb'ry   Elizabeth Boswell
  i7ii

To

Mr James Boswell of
Auchinleck Advocat
Att Edinburgh

[In another hand] : -

Auchinleck 19
Feb. 1711
Lady E.Boswell

No. 26.

My Very Dearest Heart

I wrot to you yesterday by William Smith of our little
Child John being dangerously ill, this last night blessed be
God, he got very good rest and he is much better so that
I would fain hope the worst is past, Lord give us true
thankfullness for all his mercys, and may he give us grace
to walk humblie and obediently under the sence thereof. I
am much rejoyced the time is drawing so fast on that I
hope againe to enjoy My Dearests sweet company which
I indeed much long for, Lord if it be his holy will send us
a comfortable meeting. I have time to add no more
Ocheltrie being uneasie to be gon I am

My Sweet Dearest Heart

Auchinleck   Yours most affectionatly whyle
22 Feb'ry   Elizabeth Boswell
17ii

To
Mr James Boswell of Auchin
= leck Advocat
Att Edinburgh

[in another hand] : -

Auchinleck 22
Feb'ry 1711
  Lady E. Boswell

My Very Dearest Heart

I wrot to you yesterday by William
Smith of our little Child John being dangerously ill this last night blessed be God
he got very good rest and he is much better
So that I would fain hope the worst is
past, Lord give us true thankfullness
for all his mercys, and may he give us grace
to walk humblie and obediently under the
sence therof. I am much rejoyced the time
is drawing so fast on that I hope again
to enjoy My Dearests sweet company which
I indeed much long for, Lord if it be his holy
will send us a comfortable meeting I have
time to add no more Ochiltrie being unexpe
to be gon I am

My Sweet Dearest Heart

Auchinleck   Yours most affectionatly whyle
22 Feby   Elizabeth Boswell
1711

PLATE 20 : LETTER No 26
IN ELIZABETH'S HANDWRITING

141

No. 27.

My Very Dearest Heart

I wrot this day to you with Ocheltrie but in great
heast, I take occation to salute you againe by Slouen; I
had yours by Samson just as Ocheltrie was going away,
I bless God for the continuance of your well being,
long be it so if it be his holy will. I shall take care to
send your horses the time you appoint, it is no small
refreshment to me that the time is drawing so near
that I shall hope againe enjoy my Sweet Dearests most
desireable company which much do I long for. little
Johne blessed be God continues to be better I hope
the worst is over now, the rest of the Children blessed
be God are very well, Sandie and Vetie longs much for
their dear Papa. I hope My Dearest will bring Sandies
coat with you for truly he stands much in need
thereof, he is queit growen out of his clouths. I
received all the things My Dearest mentions, and a
bottle of the Queen of Hungries water[63] my D'st
makes no mention of, I return you many thanks for
all. I wonder how Andrew Bruce could be so
extravagant to writ for so many seeds as I told him, he
said he did not think that they would have been the
half of the price, I think My Dearest has sent but to
many, Andrew Bruce says that when he bought any
seeds he allways made that in his bargaine that if the

---

(63)Queen of Hungries water; untraceable. Was it some exotic
   drink, or for medicinal purposes? With James and Elizabeth's
   frugality and canniness in mind, the later is more probable.

seeds came not up he was to pay nothing for them,
and accordingly he says one year he bought i6 ??
worth and they came not up and he pay'd not one
farthing for them, I wish My Dearest may have made
such a bargaine when you bought yours, for the last
year the most of our seeds came not up. I am truly
glad to hear that the Presidents marriage is going on
with the Lady Bangour, I hope it shall be a good
Providence for you.   I am glad My Sister is better,
poor woman Lord suport her , she has a sad husband,
he is the wholl talk here about his extravagant manner
of life whyle he was in this Countrie , Lord work a
change upon him. My Dearest always forgets to send
me holland for your necks and sleiv's I earnestly
intreat you may not forget to bring it with you, and
that you will bring also a per of slippers, for those you
have are queit gone. now My Dearest I shall trouble
you no further, Lord be with you, and send us a
comfortable meeting if it be his holy will. I am

                       My Sweet Dearest Heart
Auchinleck   Yours most affectionately whyle
22 Feb'ry 1711   Elizabeth Boswell

No. 28

My Very Dearest Sweet Heart

I shall not now trouble you with a long letter seeing I
hope so soon to be so happie of more near converse
with My Sweet Dearest which much do I long for
Lord send us a comfortable meeting if it be his holy
will little Johne blessed be God is pretty well again
Jamie has also been very ill with the cold he is better
Sandie and Vetie blessed be God are very well. I have
been much troubled with a pain in my stomach this
pretty whyle now and now I have taken the cold also
we must not always expect to be in health sickness is
also very necessary. My Lady your Mother has the cold
also very ill, your Father blessed be God is pretty well,
all remembers you with much affection and are much
rejoyced the time is so near for your return now I shall
add no more but pray God be with you and send you
a safe journey I am beyond expression

Auchinleck   Yours most affectionatly
28 Feb'ry 1711   Elizabeth Boswell

[in another hand] : -

Auchinleck 28
Febry 1711
Lady E Boswell

Chapter 6: General History

Our elder son Robert is infinitely more knowledgeable on general and indeed family history than ourselves so I am very grateful to him for the following resumé of the history of the period from the Scottish point of view:-

ACT OF UNION AND DARIEN VENTURE

The 1701 Act of Settlement (English Parliament) settled the Throne upon the House of Hanover when Queen Anne, who would succeed King William III, should die. This was deeply provocative to the Scots who passed the 1704 Security Act, delayed by James Douglas, 2nd Duke of Queensberry, the Royal Commissioner, refusing Royal Assent, but his successor John Hay 1st Marquis of Tweeddale gave assent in order to get a vital supply Bill passed. This Act reserved to the Scottish Parliament the right to nominate its own successor to the Crown, the conditions for the acceptance of the Hanoverians would be the strengthened independence of the Scottish Parliament and restrictions on the Royal Prerogative to stop the English Ministries using it to manipulate affairs in Scotland.

England feared a Stuart Monarchy and ongoing threat of invasion from the north so in an atmosphere of increasing brinkmanship, in February 1705 the

Alien Act was passed enacting that unless by September the Hanoverian succession was accepted or negotiations were entered upon for Union, Scots in England (unless domiciled) would incur penalties to make them aliens and England would close all trade in Scottish exports of cattle, linen and coal.

Ill feeling boiled over at the Alien Act and the failure of the Darien Scheme, particularly after the seizure in London of one of the Scottish company's ships, so when the ship "Worcester" was forced into Leith by bad weather it was seized in retaliation and the crew all tried for piracy on most flimsy evidence of guns being fired in an incident off the Malabar coast. With the Edinburgh mob so volatile, Captain Green, his mate and gunner were convicted and hanged on 11th April 1705, after which the riots abated and negotiations held the punitive clauses of the Alien Act in abeyance.

Some remembered the forced "Union" of Cromwell a half century earlier, the Jacobite party who desired James VIII was still significant, and many feared a Stuart restoration would overturn the benefits of the 1688-89 settlement, and provoke an English invasion, so however repugnant the loss of national independence, the Union to many was the lesser evil; whigs and presbyterians in general saw Union as less dangerous than the alternative prospect. Sir John Clerk of Penicuik, M.P. for Whithorn, expressed the confusion of views "You may see a Presbyterian minister, a Popish priest, and Episcopal prelate, all agreeing in their discourse against the Union but upon quite different views and contradictory reasons". Crowds gathered outside Parliament each day cursing and reviling the Commissioner and supporters of Union. On the night of 23rd October 1706 several hundred made for the house of Sir Pat Johnston, one of the M.P.'s for Edinburgh, previously Provost, who supported Union, they stoned windows and broke in the doors to get in but he had just escaped in time, the mob grew as it rampaged streets for several hours threatening destruction on all who promoted the Union.

Fifteen of the twenty-five Articles of Union concerned money matters; this was a period of austerity, as Lady Elizabeth's letters suggest, and poverty; the 1690's had seen disastrous harvests, and it was claimed that one in five of Edinburgh's population had died in those years; £398,000 was given to boost Scottish industry and to compensate some of the losses in the Darien scheme. The Union took effect on May 1st 1707, and legend has it that someone got into the High Kirk at St.Giles and played on the bells the tune "How Can I Be Sad Upon My Wedding Day ?"

THE DARIEN VENTURE

The last decades of the seventeenth century had seen high dividends from the East India company (chartered in December 1600), and the Hudson Bay Company (chartered 1670). In 1695 the Scottish Parliament passed the Act for the company founded to trade with "Africa and the Indies". £400,000 was raised, reckoned to be about half the capital in Scotland at the time.

Money promised to be raised in London was not forthcoming, King William and the London Parliament created obstacles to maintain the E.I.C. monopoly. William Dampier in 1679 had noted the Panama Isthmus was narrow enough to make a cross-land shortcut for trade between the two oceans. William Paterson, founding Director of the Bank of England, encouraged the venture, but only one of five ships returned to Leith and several hundred lives were lost to dysentery, and the Spanish finally expelled the colonists in March 1700. William ordered American colonies to give no aid to the Scots, so the Scots were bitter at this embargo, and blamed London for their impoverishment [Was this why Balmuto had to be sold a quarter of a century later, and why such vast debts seemed to be circulating ?]

Note: The 1701 Act of Settlement was prompted by the death of the (then) Princess Anne's only surviving child, and the natural heir; perhaps similar in setting off anxiety, to the death of Princess Charlotte over a century later.

THE WAR OF SPANISH SUCCESSION (1701 – 1713).

L ouis XIV, the Sun King, began to reign in 1643 at the age of five, the English resented his interference in seeking to induce Charles II to convert to Catholicism and later, to support the Jacobites in exile; as early as 1665 he had tried to seize what remained of the Spanish Netherlands but throughout the reign of the Hapsburg Charles II (1665-1700) in Spain, Louis' expansionism was only prevented by the intervention of England and Holland, with wars in 1667-68, 1672-78, 1683-84, and the war of the League of Augsburg, 1689-96. Spain had rival factions; the Austrian party desired Charles to be succeeded by a Hapsburg from Austria, the French party plotted for a French successor. In 1660 Louis had married the Infanta of Spain, sister to Charles so her children were the nearest relative to the throne of Spain, but would make Spain a puppet of France, creating a dangerously strong power bloc. On the death of Charles, November 1st 1700, the Duke of Anjou, grandson of Louis and Marie-Therese, became king. William III had long anticipated this and the likelihood of Louis' endangering Holland, and the Grand Alliance (League of Augsburg) was formed to back the Archduke Charles the Austrian claimant, and to counter the Franco-Spanish power bloc. Austria,

Holland, and England made up the coalition, supported also by Denmark, Portugal, and some of the German states. Louis was supported by Spain, Bavaria, and Cologne.

In 1701, England had to prepare an army, Holland on its own could only attempt to hold its borders; but the Austrians attacked Spanish possessions in the Italian Peninsula, while Louis occupied all the fortresses in the Spanish Netherlands. In 1702, Dutch armies were reinforced with English troops with John Churchill as joint Commander; he was hampered by timid Dutch deputies unwilling to let him pursue the French army, but he successfully besieged and took several forts in September and October, being created Duke of Marlborough on his return to England in November. Marlborough's attempt to take Antwerp was spoiled by inept Dutch generals, and Bavaria became the main theatre of war; the French-Bavarian-Hungarian army intended to attack Vienna but the plan collapsed. 1704 is memorable for Marlborough's Rhine and Danube campaign ending in the victory at Blenheim. 1705 saw no major moves but in 1706 there was a major victory at Ramillies in the Netherlands. In 1708, in May the French advanced to retake Brussels, Marlborough was forced to pull back before Eugene came with reinforcements, and the French swung west to retake Ghent and Bruges, and commenced to besiege Oudenarde; by a swift response Marlborough won a great victory which put the French in disorder, but

Marlborough's desire to march on Paris was forbidden. A hard winter added to France's plight but Louis withdrew from peace negotiations rather than accept harsh terms. In Spring 1709 Marlborough was once again denied his wish to move on Paris by the caution of his allies, and in June made advances in the Douai area but besieged Tournai till early September before it yielded; then close to Malplaquet there was a desperate battle, the most deperate of the war, on September 11th, which drained both armies [there is an indirect Boswell connection here; Dr. John Boswell's wife's maternal uncle, Colonel James Cranstoun, was killed in this battle; we have his portrait], and that year only Mons was taken. 1710 was fairly insignificant, with Marlborough taking no risks as the anti- Marlborough set at Court were gaining Queen Anne's confidence. In late 1711, Marlborough was ignominiously dismissed from command, and England seemed to leave the Dutch to complete the war through 1712, and before the 1713 campaign commenced the Treaty of Utrecht was signed, while in March 1714 the Treaty of Rastatt between Austria and France was signed.

In parallel with these campaigns, the joint Anglo-Dutch navy operated around the Iberian Peninsula. Admiral Sir George Rooke won a victory at Cadiz on October 12th 1702, in 1703 Portugal joining the allies opened Lisbon for use as a base. Admiral Sir Clowdisley Shovel returning late in the year lost many ships in the Great Storm of November 27th [in which the original Eddystone Lighthouse was washed away, and the Bishop of Bath and Wells and his wife were killed by the falling of a chimney of the Bishop's Palace]. Also in 1703, with Admiral Byng bombarding from seaward and 1800 marines landing behind to cut off the Spanish fort, Gibraltar was captured; and Barcelona after a lengthy siege, on October 3rd; the French then sent forces which besieged until the following April 30th when they were forced to abandon siege. Leaving Barcelona safely held, Admiral Leake continued, to take Cartagena, Alicante, Mallorca and Ibiza, while troops advancing from Lisbon took Madrid on June 29th. Sir Clowdisley Shovel was lost in returning with twelve ships of the line when several were wrecked on the Isles of Scilly on October 27th 1707. In August 1708 Admiral Leake took Sardinia, with Minorca falling to General Stanhope the following month. In 1710, Stanhope moved the Austrian Charles to Madrid but was forced to retreat later in the year; and at Brihuego on December 9th the Franco-Spanish forces won a victory and captured Stanhope, driving the allies back to Barcelona which they held until the Peace of Utrecht of 1713.

RELIGIOUS BACKGROUND

The eighteenth century opened as a turbulent period drew to a close; those of adult years would have lived through the period known in Scotland as the "Killing Time" in the 1680's. For half a century the Presbyterian church had suffered oppression from the authoritarian Stuart kings, and many people had given up their liberty or life rather than yield their convictions. The settlement of 1690 secured the Presbyterian church, and in the Act of Union of 1707 the Scots ensured full protection for the continuance of an independent Church and legal system, but living through such days would have kindled a fervent zeal. South-west Scotland had been the arena for more of the strife than any other part of Scotland, and it was brought to Auchinleck in 1686 when the Covenanter the Rev. Alexander Peden, having been sick, and in hiding locally, died. He was son of a laird in the next parish of Sorn and the two families had a longstanding friendship. By the 1680's Alexander's brother Hugh Peden was a tenant of David Boswell's on the Auchinleck estate and it was here the "Prophet of the Covenant" resorted as his health finally failed, hiding out in a cave beside the Lugar little more than a mile down from Auchinleck Old House, his family bringing him provisions until he grew weak and went to his brother's house for his final two days, his life ending on 26th January. Upon learning of his death, David Boswell, by some accounts, secreted the body in the family's own vault. However the resting place was discovered within six weeks and "Poor Auld Sandie" was disinterred by dragoons for public display on the gallows, and later burial there, in Cumnock, despite the protestations of David. As a young lad growing up with such events transpiring around him, it is inconceivable that James would not have been influenced in his outlook.

1685 had seen the infamous Revocation by Louis XIV of the religious liberties of French Huguenots granted in the 1598 Edict of Nantes and refugees in large numbers had arrived in England, and their presence and accounts of the ongoing persecution of their brethren still in France would have been a continuing reminder of their own recently ended turmoil.

Many of the Huguenots were traders and artisans in a slowly emerging middle class; those who fled brought industries such as lacemaking to Britain, and the suppression of the potential middle class through the eighteenth century was a major factor leading up to the French Revolution, whereas a growing middle class and the opportunity for the escape from poverty prevented the same extremism emerging in Britain.

Robert D. Boswell

Based on information from : -

    "Encyclopaedia of Scotland"
    "History of Auchinleck"   Dane Love
    "Edinburgh"   Alan Massie
    "Men of the Covenant"   Alexander Smellie

Letters No. J 1 – J 3 (1733)

Letter No. J 1

My Dear John   Edinburgh
Jan'ry 30

1733

It is not want of affection that I have been so long
without writing to you which I hope you do me the
justice to believe, I am glad to hear you are better
which I hope will still be so till you arrive to the
perfect day, tho as long as we are in this world we may
be still laying our account with clouds, now and then,
which when the sun shins againe makes it the more
pleasant, and when those clouds comes againe, we
should remember the days when we were inluminat
and not cast away our confidence, read Heb:i0 Ch:
ve:35, Heb: 3 Ch: ve 6 and i4, our faith should not
stand upon fraims, but upon the Rock Christ Jesus,
and ther we should build, wher tho the rains descend
and floods come and the winds blow and beat upon
that house it shall not fall being founded upon the
Rock Christ, as he has told us Mathew Ch:7 ve 24 &
25. My Dearest son I shall say no more being very
unfitt for writing upon so high a matter but what I
have writ I bless God I have some experience of tho
to my shame I come farr short to Gods goodness to
me. but I desire and ther is only our safety, while in
this wilderness to be leaning upon our Beloved Christ

who of God is made unto us wisdom Rightousness
Sanctification and Redemption
I am glad Dear John you are in good company Mr
Cuni[n]gham is a worthy Man your Brother James is
much better he took the jandice after his great illness,
but is also better of that. both your Brothers has
themselves kindly remember'd to you receive the book
you wrot for, I think you are much in the right to
follow bussiness. I have not Thomas a Kempis here it
is at Auchinleck. receive powder and a pluff in your
leather bag, receive also oyll.

farewell Dear John in heart I remaine
                              Your affectionat Mother
pray offer my very   Eli: Boswell
kind and humble
service to Mr Cunigham
and Mrs Cunigham

[on other side] : -

I have given the bearer a shillen I had
derected all to Mr Cunigham because I would not
have people know wher you are

                To
Mr John Boswell student of
Physick

                Att Smalham

Hebrews: 10 : 35 ; "Cast not away therefore your confidence,which hath great compensation of reward."

Hebrews:3 : 6 ; " But Christ as a son over his own house; whose house are we, if we hold fast the confidence and the rejoicing of the hope firm unto the end."

Hebrews 3: 14 ;" For we are made partakers of Christ, if we hold the beginning of our confidence stedfast unto the end; "

Matthew : 7 : 24, 25 ; " Therefore whosoever heareth these sayings of mine, and doeth them, I will liken him unto a wise man, which built his house upon a rock : And the rain descended, and the floods came, and the winds blew, and beat upon that house; and it fell not : for it was founded upon a rock."

No. J 2.

My Dear John   Edinburgh   July 4
                                 1733

I expected to hear from you yesterday as I use to do, the reason I suspect that the Man has not call'd you use to send with, that I hear he was very ill pleased with what he got for his pains as they told me after he was gon, tho he got a shillen, he having severall drougs to take out he alledged it was so little, he got a shillen the week befor for the same reason, Dear John I cannot imagine what use you make of so many drougs which no doubt comes to a vast soum of mony I am told near nein pound stairlen I hope you have the prudence to get payment for them from them you give them to, that you take nothing for your pains till you come from abroad I shall say nothing, but if you do not make them pay for their drougs is most ridiculous, yea further I say it would be unjustice, you know my Dear you have nothing but what you have from your Father, who has anough ado with what he has, and has labour'd and does labour not a little for his Children, other ways he would not have now to give you and the rest, But then they should endeavour not to add to his charges by unnecessary expence, to be sure he must be at considerable charge for your education abroad, which he will be very farr from grudging what is necessary, you have reason to bless God for such a Father, that both has to give, and also has the will, but then his Childrens duty is as I said befor not to add to his charge by unnecessary

expence, if you had a great estate you might do with
your own what you pleased, but as it is other ways, and
in your circumstances, ther is no prudence, nor
religone not to take mony for your drougs, but much
to the contrary, we are requier'd indeed to love mony,
but first to do justice, if it please God to preserve you,
and bless you in your imployment, I hope Dear John,
you may be in a condition to do a great deal of good,
and charitie to the poor, But believe me if you naither
take for your pains nor payment for your drougs you
cannot expect to be usefull to the poor, but to be ane
object yourself of charitie, unless it wer by way of
miracle which we are not to expect.But I have said to
much on this subject, for when I consider I cannot
think you are so foolish (as I may well call it) not to
take payment for your drougs, especially from those
that may well pay, this is not charity, but a degree of
prid, if you rightly examine into the matter you will
find it to be so, our heart is very deceitfull, therefore
My Dear we have great reason to pray search and try
me and lead me in the right path. I hope by your nixt
you will give me some satisfieing account about your
taking payment for the drougs so that befor you go
abroad you will send the mony to pay for them. I shall
add no more at this time I continue
                    Dear John
                Your affectionat Mother
                    Eli: Boswell

[on other part of sheet] : -

Since my letter on the other syde was wrot I received
yours I am glad to hear you continue well blessed be
God I have time tosay no more at this time but receive
two dozen of Mr Baits pens and a per threed stockens
and a loaf and your linens as Mrs M^c crone will
informe you your Father and all here remembers you
affectionatly I am

      Your affectionat mother
        Eli: Boswell

No. J 3.

My Dear John

I had the pleasure of yours, and it is not a small refreshment to me to hear of your being so well every way, blessed be our good God, may he continue it if it be his holy will. I gave your Uncle your inclosed letter, who took it very kindly your concern for his Child in writing derections for her, but she is now beyond needing help for it has pleased God to remove her monday evening last, she was buried upon tusday. Your uncle has brought over his Lady the day after to devert her, poor woman it is havie upon her being the first breatch of her little flock, but bears it very Christianly, she is vastly thine[thin?].We have been inquest about Mr Black, but cannot learn when he is to be in toun, I am affraid you will not have the benefit of going alongs with him, unless you would stay longer than it seems you have inclination, ther is a shipp going from Lith to Holland the 28 of this month, tomorrow eight days, they say a very good ship, and discreit Skipper, and a gentleman is going alongs ane acquaintance of Mistres Ker who she commends much, so Dear John I think you may imbrass this occasion, which if you do you may come here I think upon thursday nixt week. I received what you mention and shall

take care to put all up and get what you desire farewell
My Dear Son in heast I continue
Edinburgh   Your affectionat Mother
July 20 :1733   Eli : Boswell

                    To
        Mr John Boswell Student of
        Physick for present
        Att Smellhome

Epilogue

Lady Elizabeth died in 1739, just before the birth of the biographer, her grandson. One can only surmise what influence she might have exerted on him. He often wrote of his grandfather whom he knew for about nine years. Such is the quirk of history.

Ramsay of Ochtertyre makes an interesting inference in his section on Lord Auchinleck. Discussing James senior he states : -

> p.160, "He married a daughter of the Earl of Kincardine by a Dutch lady of noble family. For this, however it would appear his posterity paid dear, for most of them had peculiarities for which they had better have wanted---" and in connection with James junior's support for the Douglas cause, p.173, " His behaviour on that occasion savoured so much of insanity, that it was generally imputed to his Dutch blood."

Could this be an early example of what today would be called racism ? Certainly Elizabeth shows no sign of mental problems in her correspondence, indeed one could say she demonstrates considerable intelligence and understanding in her dealings with the Kirk and Ministerial succession, and in handling estate business. It has to be agreed that some family members had peculiarities, for example James the elder twin, whom we learnt had mental problems before he died, and his brother John my ancestor was considered eccentric in his later life, but then so are many of us!

Now for an item of personal history. Apart from immediate family members, not many will be aware that, in a similar manner to Alexander, Lord Auchinleck, as revealed by this group of letters, I have succeeded to the "Auchinleck" genealogical title through the death of an elder brother, presenting a personal "what if ?" situation. He was Arthur Legh, born in 1924, three years before myself, and named after our maternal grandfather, Arthur Thomas Hunter, and our paternal great uncle, William Legh, younger brother of Henry St. George mentioned earlier. At the age of nineteen he entered the Royal Air Force for wartime service, with the ambition of becoming a navigator. However on undergoing his "medical" for this, radiographs revealed lymph glands in the chest which were diagnosed as being due to leukaemia, and sadly he died from this after only a few months. September 11th has been a memorial date for my family since 1943. With modern drugs and treatment, no doubt he would have had a good chance of survival. The sole reason I bring this up is that having written this little book to publish Lady Elizabeth's most interesting letters, I propose to donate any profits to cancer research in his memory.

Bibliography

James Boswell;   The Journal of a tour to the Hebrides with
                  Samuel Johnson, Ll.D.
T.Cadell & W. Davies, London, 1807

David Buchanan; The Treasure of Auchinleck; The Story of the
                  Boswell Papers.
Heinemann, London, 1975

Anne Buck;   Clothes and the Child; A Handbook of
                  .Childrens' Dress in England, 1500-.1900.
Ruth Bean, Bedford, 1996.

Burke's Landed Gentry of Great Britain, 19th Edition;
                  The Kingdom in Scotland;
Stokesley, North Yorkshire,2001.

Collins Encyclopaedia of Scotland;
Ed. by John Keay and Julia Keay;
HarperCollinsPublishers, 1994.

Roger Craik;   James Boswell (1740-1795), The .Scottish
                  Perspective; The Faculty of Advocates,
                  Edinburgh;
H.M.S.O., 1994.

Sir William A. Craigie;   A Dictionary of the Older Scottish
                  Tongue from 12th to end of. 17th Centuries;
O.U.P., London,1937. [noted as S.D.(C.).]

BIBLIOGRAPHY

C.Willett and Phyllis C. Cunnington; Handbook of English
Costume in the Eighteenth.Century;
Plays Inc., Boston, 1972.

David Daiches;   James Boswell and his World;
Thames and Hudson, 1976.

Dictionary of National Biography;
Smith Elder and Co., London, 1890.

Encyclopaedia Brittanica; ?1890

Encyclopaedia of Antiques;
Octopus Books Ltd., 1976.

Fasti Ecclesiae Scoticanae, Vol. III, Synod of Glasgow and Ayr;
Oliver and Boyd, Edinburgh, 1920.

Gray's Anatomy;
Longmans Green, London, 1877.

John Jamieson;   A Dictionary of the Scottish Language;
William Tait, Edinburgh, 1846. [noted as S.D.(J.)].

Robert Lomas;   The Invisible College; The Royal
Society,Freemasonry, and the Birth of Modern
Science
BCA, 2002

Dane Love;   The History of Auchinleck – Village and
                 Parish;
Carn Publishing, Cumnock,1991.

Allan Massie;   Edinburgh;
Sinclair Stevenson,1994.

Needlework Dictionary, Pamela Clabborn, 1976
MacMillen, London, 1976.

New Shell Guide to Scotland; Ed.by Donald Lamond Macnie
                 from the original by Moray MacLaren.
Ebury Press, 1978.

F.A.Pottle;   James Boswell: The Earlier Years (1740- 1769);
Heinemann, London, 1966.

C.Ryskamp and F.A.Pottle;   James Boswell:
                 The Ominous Years (1774 – 1776);
Heinemann, London,

David Ross;   Scottish Place-names;
Birlinn Limited, 2001.

Alexander Smellie;   Men of the Covenant;
Edinburgh: Banner of Truth, 1975

T.C. Smout;   A History of the Scottish People, .
                 1560 – 1830
FontanaPress/Harper Collins, 1985.

Index

CONTENTS

INDEX